WHERE IS JESUS?

An in-depth look into the Church of Jesus
Christ of Latter Day Saints

WHERE IS JESUS?

An in-depth look into the Church of Jesus
Christ of Latter-day Saints

Written by:
Brenton Laidler

Published by:
Brenton Laidler

Cover art:
Brenton Laidler & Lila Elizabeth

Cover model:
Alex Peacock

3rd Edition

Copyright © 2014 by Brenton Laidler

First Printing: 2014

ISBN 978-1-312-70367-4

The Church of Jesus Christ of Latter-day Saints uses the King James Version of the Bible. As such, all Biblical quotations are from the KJV unless otherwise specified.

For more information, please visit

www.WhereIsJesusBook.com
WhereIsJesusBlog.blogspot.com
www.facebook.com/needtofindHim

or email me at WhereIsJesusBook@gmail.com

For my wife and kids.
I love you.

TABLE OF CONTENTS

Introduction

"*For I am not ashamed of the gospel, because it is the power of God that brings salvation to everyone who believes: first to the Jew, then to the Gentile.*"

- Romans 1:16

A Little Background on Me

I was raised in the Church of Jesus Christ of Latter-day Saints and was a member until the age of twenty-one. In January of 2007 I decided to leave the LDS church and commit my life to Christ. Since then, I have been asked by a number of my friends to share my conversion story. Some asked because they wanted to hear how God moved in my life. Others wanted to know if my conversion was genuine. I can tell you it was genuine, but I fought Him every step of the way. It took years for my stubborn heart to turn to Him. Thankfully, I eventually found myself in the arms of His ever abundant grace. If you would like to read my entire conversion story, please flip to the last chapter of this book. As you read it, my hope is that you focus on God's faithful hand in my life and notice the power of His furious love. For those who are soldiering on and continuing to read, just know that Jesus is everything to me. I believe that He has made everything and that He is sovereign over everything. Rest assured, He and I have a strong and healthy relationship.

Throughout these past few years I have found that many of my Christian friends have a lot of questions regarding Mormon theology. For a while, it seemed like I was being constantly asked to share what I knew about and how I was raised within the Mormon Church. Questions like, "What are the differences between what Mormons believe and what we believe?" and "What's the deal with their underwear?" seemed to be a weekly occurrence. Oddly enough, it was not just my new church family that had questions. A few of my Mormon friends would still ask me things like, "What made you leave?" or "Have your beliefs really changed all that much?" I was even asked, "Do you ever see yourself getting baptized and re-joining the

Mormon Church?" I tried to answer both sides the best I could but I never felt as though I had enough information. I soon found myself constantly researching Mormon theology so to better equip myself to answer these tough questions. This book is the result of that research.

I almost feel like I know more about the LDS church now than I ever did when I was a member. But do not think of me as all-knowing. I, by no means, consider myself an expert in LDS doctrine. I do, however, know what I was taught growing up in the church, what I have been told by countless missionaries and members, and what I have read on official LDS websites, blogs, publications, and in their scriptures. With that being said, I would still encourage you to check my facts, my sources, and do your own research should you feel the need.

I wanted to take a moment and speak directly to some of my friends and family. I want you all to know that this book was no easy task. I am not referring to the amount work and time it took me to write it, although it was substantial. I say this because I know of the potential impact this book can have on not only your life and your family's lives, but also on our relationship. Some of you have been my closest friends since before high school. Some of you are coworkers or past coworkers. Others are part of my immediate or extended family. For some, I was around when you met your wife or husband. I was fortunate enough to hold your newborn baby, and you were there for me when I needed a friend. God has truly blessed me with thousands upon thousands of memories with you amazing and wonderful people. The thought of losing any of you in my life is almost unbearable. I hope and pray that you understand that what I say in these pages I felt called by God to say. I know many of you have very solid roots in the church and are very content in your religion. You may read my words and perceive them as a blatant attack on something you hold so dear. Please know that my heart was filled with nothing but love and I thought of each of you while writing every word.

I also need you all to know that my goal in writing this book was never to coax anyone to leave their home church. Understand that I am not concerned with where you park your car on Sunday mornings. That is a secondary issue in my book (no pun intended). Neither was my goal to somehow start a movement to abolish Mormonism from the face of the earth. The only thing I care about is that your life is Christ-centered.

With that being said, the fact of the matter still remains. God has placed it on my heart to write this book and so I did. So, while my heart's desire is not to invite conflict or strain on an already difficult relationship my life must be first and foremost about Jesus. It would be hypocritical of me to write this book and not live it myself.

How It All Got Started

There was one moment in particular in my adolescence that was pivotal in my relationship with God. It was a sunny afternoon – a bit cliché, but true none the less – and I was on a car ride with my father and my brother. My brother had just returned home from his LDS mission a few months back and I was eagerly watching his faith develop. Being that he was my older brother, it was only natural that I looked up to him and emulated him. Although I had been born and raised in the Mormon Church, I still had doubts, struggles, and hesitations. My faith was not as strong as it could be. When I saw how strong my brother was, it gave me purpose. If he was confident in the faith then I knew I could be as well. He was my rock, so to speak. However, on that day, during that one particular car ride, I remember hearing how truly shaky my brother's faith really was. He was telling us both that his mission did not actually help his faith, but rather made him question it.

Now, I do not remember everything that was said that day, in fact, probably very few specifics except for one. I remember the story my brother told about one of the times he was going door to door with a new missionary. He said there was this one house in particular where a very nice woman opened the door. They chatted for a while and invited her to church. As they approached the end of their exchange, my brother took the lead. To close, he decided to bare his testimony. According to my brother, he had given her the perfect text book testimony. He said that had it been said in church, every mother in the congregation would have been "throwing their daughters at him." Again those are his words, not mine. After he had finished, the lady smiled at him and thanked him for his genuine words. Then, with such sincerity, she responded,

"That's great and all, but where does Jesus fit in?"

My brother was at a loss for words. It was in that moment that he realized that not once did he mention or acknowledge Jesus. He tried to backtrack and explain himself but it was too late. She had heard enough and was uninterested in anything else they had to say.

To this day, this story fascinates me. The fact that my brother, the faithful LDS member, the one that I looked up to, asked questions and regarded as being my spiritual compass, who was seemingly doing everything 'right' by the LDS standard, was found wanting really impacted me. From that point on, I began to focus more and more on the motives behind my faith, but no matter where my search took me I never forgot how important Jesus should be.

Through my research, God has given me the opportunity to really meet and talk with some amazing people. It has opened doors to people in places that I would normally never have the opportunity to discuss deep, theological matters. One of these instances happened with a Mormon coworker of mine not too long ago.

He told me about a time that he was with a group of people from all different religions in a prayer circle. They each had a turn to pray for a production that they were putting together. He said that not once, in hearing their cries to God, did he think that a certain prayer was unheard. He took a good look around the circle and could honestly feel a sense of camaraderie with these believers. After their prayer time he had a conversation with one of these men from the circle. It was in this conversation that this person basically told my friend that since he was Mormon he was not a Christian.

"I was hurt," said my friend who expressed deep sorrow for having someone he respected so much attack his beliefs. "I know we have some differences but our main belief, the core of what we focus on, is the same. Who is he to say that he was a Christian but I was not?" His frustration and sorrow could be easily seen.

Obviously this was not the first conversation I have had with this friend. I have heard his heart and, while it is not for me to judge or decide, I can attest that his heart is truly pointed to Jesus. I know that he loves Christ with all his heart and his personal beliefs and actions reflect that love. So when the topic of his Christianity came into question, I felt obligated to respond.

I told him, first and foremost, that I could see his heart and that I could tell that he really loved the Savior. I then told him to brace himself, because what I was about to say would be the hardest pill to swallow. I told him that though his personal focus was on Jesus, the LDS church does not share that focus. The LDS church's doctrine, the majority of its people, and what I was taught as a younger man exemplify this. I continued by telling him that the reason most people, myself included, do not perceive Mormons as Christian is because of their Jesus. I humbly told him that the biblical Jesus and the Mormon Jesus were not the same. I then quoted Matthew where Jesus warns us of false messiahs (Matt. 24:24) and that not all who claim to know Jesus will be recognized by Him when the end comes (Matt. 7:21-23).

I then asked if he ever noticed that whenever people share their testimony in church – which is every 1st Sunday of every month – Jesus is rarely spoken of. I told him that I started paying attention to this fact back when I was still attending the LDS church and, to me, it felt like Jesus had become an afterthought. When *any* church does that, that church is no longer worth attending.

This, and many other experiences like it, is why I felt impressed enough to write this book. It is designed to get you to focus on one thing and one thing only: Jesus. Where is Jesus? It is a simple question with a very powerful answer. I truly believe that all other religious discussions pale in comparison to the topic of Jesus Christ. Sadly, not enough people seem to agree with me. It is a sad reality that all too often our Lord and Savior is overlooked. It is exponentially worse when this happens as a result of following a church. I hope that wherever you call home, whatever religion you classify yourself as, Jesus is being preached. My prayer is that this book will encourage you to examine your current relationship with Him and maybe bring you closer to His throne.

Section One: Christianity

"As a church, we have critics—many of them. They say we do not believe in the traditional Christ of Christianity. There is some substance to what they say. Our faith, our knowledge, is not based on ancient tradition...Our faith, our knowledge comes of the witness of a prophet in this dispensation."

-Gordon B. Hinckley
15th President of the Church of Jesus Christ of Latter Day Saints
April 2002 General Conference

What Do You Mean
When You Say Jesus?

Naturally, before we can answer the title question of "Where is Jesus?" we must accurately define who He is. Throughout history there have been many different types of Jesuses that have come up. For instance, in the Muslim Faith Jesus is a great prophet, born of a virgin by the power of God but He is not God personified. In Judaism, Jesus was considered a false messiah who led millions of people astray. The Baha'is believe Jesus was just another manifestation of God in a series of personages reciting God's message to the world but who had no divinity. Buddhists believe that Jesus did not die on the cross but instead traveled to India and was the prophet Yuz Asaf.[1] I, myself, am a firm believer in the authority of the Bible and therefore take the mainstream Christian perspective that Jesus is, in fact, the true Messiah.

The question then of which Jesus we should worship is not a new one. Nor is this subject overlooked in the Bible. For thousands of years, the Bible has warned us to be watchful of false messiahs. *"For there shall arise false Christs, and false prophets, and shall shew great signs and wonders; insomuch that, if it were possible, they shall deceive the very elect"* (Matt. 24:24). It would seem that uncovering the identity of the true Jesus is a very critical issue. Graciously, God has given us the resources to check our facts to ensure our praise goes to the One who deserves it.

At face value, the Church of Jesus Christ of Latter-day Saints seems to have the same Jesus as most other mainstream Bible believing churches do. He was born to a virgin mother. He had twelve apostles and performed many miracles throughout

---

[1] "Religious perspectives on Jesus," Wikipedia. www.wikipedia.org (Accessed 27 June 2014)

His life. He was falsely accused, tried, beaten, and unjustly condemned to die on a cross. He then conquered death and was raised three days later, showing Himself to hundreds of people and thereby establishing His authority and dominion over this world. It is here that most preliminary discussions with LDS members regarding the person of Jesus end. This leads people to believe that mainstream Christianity and Mormonism have the same Jesus. You may even be one of those people.

What may surprise you then is that when Mormons say Jesus, or God, or even the Holy Spirit (or Ghost) their meaning is actually completely different. From a doctrinal standpoint, topics such as the nature of Jesus, His origins, the Holy Trinity, and the gift of salvation are just as different from mainstream Christianity as are the above religions. These differences, while seemingly innocent extensions of Biblical testimony, are dangerously misleading.

Jesus is, without a doubt, the most important person that ever walked the face of this earth. It is because of the magnitude of His life that we must be sure that the Jesus we worship is the actual Jesus who deserves it. We must be sure that everything we believe about Jesus, including His life, His ministry, His message, His origins, etc. is completely true and accurate. Otherwise, our beliefs and His gospel are meaningless.

Let me put it this way. Have you ever Googled yourself? I have. I once typed my name in the search bar and to my amazement I found another Brenton Laidler. Oddly enough, after a few emails back and forth and getting to know him as a person, I discovered that we are actually very similar. We are the same age, both active Christians, have coached sports, and have been married for just about the same amount of time. To be honest, I was a bit taken back with the amount of similarities between us. It was uncanny. If I were famous, this could be very confusing for some people. Mistaken identity is not an uncommon problem, especially in the information age. How much worse do you think it is for the Savior of the World?

The point I am trying to make is that there is at least more than one 'Brenton Laidler' in the world. Luckily if you get either of us confused, not much harm will come of it. Maybe a few confusing emails back and forth but nothing serious. However, when it comes to the person of Jesus Christ, if you worship anyone other than the One the Holy Bible speaks of, the consequences will be much more severe.

The Other Brother
of Jesus

The LDS Doctrine makes a very unique claim about the origin of Jesus. They claim that Jesus is not only our literal spiritual brother, but the brother of Satan, who is Lucifer, the devil.

> The Father is understood to be the literal father of His spirit children. ...God the Father also had many other spirit children, created in His image and that of His Only Begotten. These children include all humans born on the earth. Some of God's children rebelled against Him, and contested the choice of Jesus as Savior. (See D&C 76:25–27). The leader of these children was Lucifer, or Satan. Those spirit children of God who followed Satan in his rebellion against Christ are sometimes referred to as "demons," or "devils." (See Moses 4:1–4, Abraham 3:24–28). Thus, it is technically true to say that Jesus and Satan are "brothers," in the sense that both have the same spiritual parent, God the Father.[2]

According to Mormon beliefs, we existed before our time here on earth in a state called the Pre-mortal existence. (This is a point that I will cover in more detail in section two of this book. In this section, however, I would like to keep our focus primarily on the idea that Jesus and Satan have the same spiritual parent). During the creation of the world, God the Father parented Jesus, Lucifer, the angels, and the entire human race and we all dwelt with Him in the pre-mortal state of existence.

---

[2] "Jesus Christ/Brother of Satan: Children of God,"
http://en.fairmormon.org/Jesus_Christ/Brother_of_Satan, (November 28, 2013)

Mormons claim that Jesus is our eldest brother, He is the firstborn (D&C 93:21), and thus making Lucifer one of Jesus' little brothers.

Mormon doctrine also claims that both Jesus and Lucifer had a redemptive plan for mankind. God wanted *"to see if [mankind would] do all the things whatsoever the Lord their God shall command them...And the Lord said: Whom shall I send? And one answered like unto the Son of Man: Here am I, send me. And another answered and said: Here am I, send me. And the Lord said: I will send the first. And the second was angry, and kept not his first estate; and, at that day, many followed after him"* (Abr. 3:25, 27-28). According to Mormonism, God the Father chose Jesus' plan for redemption over Lucifer's. This, in turn, caused Lucifer to be angry with God the Father and Jesus. It is because of this supernatural sibling rivalry that Lucifer was eventually cast out of Heaven and became Satan.

In addition to this rivalry between the two, the LDS church has also implied that Jesus was a created being. Since we have a beginning, it is then safe to assume that so would our oldest brother. As Mormonism claims we were created in the pre-mortal existence, we therefore can assert that so were all of our siblings, which includes Jesus. As such, Jesus is not eternal. Mormons, by default, believe and teach that Jesus did in fact have a beginning. They do, however, believe that He has no end. The Book of Mormon teaches that after His death and resurrection He was seated at the right hand of God forever and ever (Moroni 7:27 & 9:26).

The Holy Trinity

The very first statement of faith of the Mormon Church is *"We believe in God, the eternal father, and in His son, Jesus Christ, and in the Holy Ghost"* (Articles of Faith 1:1). This statement seems to coincide perfectly with the Bible. However, we must not simply take these words at face value. We need to understand that there is a major difference between what mainstream Christians hear and what Mormons actually believe.

Stephen Edward Robinson, a religious scholar and apologist for the LDS church, states in one of his publications, "What Latter-day Saints do not believe is...the doctrine that God is three coequal persons in one substance or essence. We do not believe it because it is not scriptural."[3] Furthermore, the "LDS doctrine does not subscribe to traditional creedal trinitarianism. That is, the LDS do not believe the extra-biblical doctrines which surround many Christians' ideas about God, such as expressed by the Nicene Creed. Specifically, the LDS do not accept the proposition that Jesus Christ and the Holy Spirit are 'of one substance (homoousios) with the Father...Rather, LDS doctrine teaches that God the Father is physically and personally distinct from Jesus Christ, His Only Begotten Son.'"[4]

In actuality then, the first Article of Faith could end with "...and believe them to be three separate beings." At face value, this first article of faith is deceptively familiar for most mainstream Bible believers. However, it is actually saying something very contrary to their belief. It instead immediately

---

[3] Stephen E. Robinson, "Are Mormons Christians?" https://www.lds.org, (May, 1998)
[4] "Jesus Christ/Brother of Satan: Children of God,"
http://en.fairmormon.org/Jesus_Christ/Brother_of_Satan, (November 28, 2013)

makes a distinction between God the Father, Jesus, and the Holy Spirit as being three separate beings. In addition, it needs to be understood that when the majority of Mormons say God, they are only referring to God the Father and not to anyone else.

The beloved prophet Joseph Smith taught, "I will preach on the plurality of Gods...I have always declared...Jesus Christ a separate and distinct personage from God the Father, and that the Holy Ghost was a distinct personage and a Spirit: and these three constitute three distinct personages and three Gods."[5] This is why Mormons are categorized as polytheists, or believers in multiple gods. Joseph Smith, Brigham Young, and other LDS prophets and apostles often taught on the plurality of gods. In addition to these Gods, many Mormons believe that their eternal purpose is to one day become a God themselves.

To my LDS friends that are reading this and are conflicted with the idea of polytheism, allow me to expound. This is more for your understanding than anything else. Though you may only claim to worship one God, there is still a belief in the existence of multiple gods. Joseph Smith said himself there are at least "three Gods" in the Heavens. Therefore, if anyone believes that even more than one God exists, regardless of where they reside or whether or not they have a direct influence on anyone's life, they are by definition a polytheist. Mainstream Christianity, on the other hand, is defined as a monotheistic belief system. They believe that the Father, Jesus, and the Holy Spirit are literally one God. Again, it is not a belief that the Father, the Son, and the Holy Spirit have the same purpose, or that They are merely one in unity. Mainstream Christians believe that within the nature of God there are three manifestations, but are all reflections of one almighty God.

---

[5] Joseph Smith Jr. and Joseph Fielding Smith, *Teachings of the Prophet Joseph Smith*, (Deseret Book Company, 1938), 370.

His Work on the Cross

Christ died on the cross for our sins. It is His blood that atones for our iniquities and allows us to be with Him one day. I want the reader to know that this fact is neither disputed nor overlooked within the LDS church. They too claim that Christ's work on the cross is pivotal to an eternal life with him.

However, the impact of that atonement is very different. Mormons believe that salvation is free to all mankind, but only after you have done everything you can to earn it. *"For we labor diligently to write, to persuade our children, and also our brethren, to believe in Christ, and to be reconciled to God; for we know that it is by grace that we are saved, after all we can do"* (2 Nephi 25:23). Salvation then is not based on grace, but by works.

Growing up in the church, whenever the subject of salvation arose, there was a story that was used to better explain the phrase *"after all we can do."* Pretend that you are an eight year old kid and you want a bike. Your dad tells you that at the end of the month he will take you to the store so that you can buy one. Knowing that you do not have enough money to buy it yet, you begin to do as many chores around the house as you can. You may even mow a few lawns around the neighborhood to earn a few extra bucks just to be safe. When the end of the month comes, you walk in the store confident knowing you have worked and saved all you could. However, when the clerk rings up the bike it is painfully obvious you do not have enough money. With your head now heavy, you bow your head and begin to cry. Your dad, seeing your grief and knowing how hard you worked, steps in and says, "Child, because I love you so much I will make you a deal. You give me all the money you saved and a kiss on my cheek and I will buy that bike for you." Your father sees your heart and steps in and makes up the difference. Had you not worked so hard your father would have known you really did not want the bike and would not have paid the difference.

God is the obvious metaphorical father in this story which teaches kids that He sees our efforts, knows our hearts, and when the time comes He will step in to make up the difference. Salvation then, in the LDS church, is something that can be earned. For even if only a slight attempt is made, the LDS church is teaching its members they have to try, to work, so that their 'Father' will see their efforts.

The money that the child earns is a metaphor for the things that need to be done on this earth for salvation. The LDS church refers to these acts as ordinances. "*We believe that through the Atonement of Christ, all mankind may be saved, by obedience to the laws and ordinances of the Gospel*" (Articles of Faith 1:3). The next logical question would be, "What are these ordinances we must follow in order to be saved?" Essentially, how can I earn some money for that bike? For that answer, we have to go to the next article of faith, which says, "*We believe that the first principles and ordinances of the Gospel are: first, Faith in the Lord Jesus Christ; second, Repentance; third baptism by immersion for the remission of sins; fourth, Laying on of hands for the gift of the Holy Ghost*" (Articles of Faith 1:4).

What these two Articles are saying is that there are multiple criteria that must be completed in order to receive salvation, in addition to the blood of Jesus. However, what is not being explained is that being baptized and having hands laid on you to receive the Holy Spirit are just the first of many ordinances that must be followed. In addition, LDS members are to be married in the temple, be faithful tithe payers, and follow the word of wisdom. They must also attend church regularly, agree to serve on a mission, and do all of their home teaching.

A while back, I remember having a conversation with a member of the LDS church about the idea of salvation by works.

He told me that Heaven was like a beautiful gated community. Our sin had caused God to create an incredibly tall fence that no one and nothing could get past. However, when Jesus died on the cross the gates on that fence opened up and left a gap wide enough for us to walk through. He then said that walking through that gate is a metaphor for the work we do on earth. We take a step each time we pay our tithe, do our home teaching, go to church, follow the word of wisdom, get married in the temple, get baptized, and become priesthood holders. My friend said very plainly, "Jesus opened the door, but we have to walk through it."

Who Does the Bible
Say Jesus Is?

Are Jesus and Satan brothers? We must always refer to His Holy Word for answers. In Colossians, Paul says of Jesus, *"For by him were all things created, that are in heaven, and that are in earth, visible and invisible, whether they be thrones, or dominions, or principalities, or powers: all things were created by him, and for him"* (Col. 1:16). We then, as well as everything else in this world, including the angels, were created by Jesus. Even the apostle John says that it is through Jesus that all things were made (John 1:3). Is the gardener related to anything he grows in the garden? How could the architect be the brother of what he builds? The same is with God. Since Satan is a creation of Jesus, He and Satan cannot possibly be brothers. The bold claim that Jesus, our Creator and Savior, is the brother of Satan goes against the very foundation of the Bible. It not only challenges the biblical account of creation but also the very nature of Jesus Himself.

Furthermore, the implication that Jesus is a created being is extremely unbiblical. The Bible says that Jesus is the Alpha and the Omega, the beginning and the end (Rev. 22:13). He is not a creation, but the Creator. Jesus personally addressed the subject of His eternal nature in the book of John. *"Jesus said to them, "Verily, Verily I say unto you, before Abraham was, I am"* (John 8:58). Linguistically speaking, Jesus states that He has always existed. On this there can be no debate.

The Holy Trinity is a doctrine that can be a very challenging concept to grasp. We must, however, cling to the truths given in scripture stating that God the Father, Jesus, and the Holy Spirit are in fact one (John 10:30). This is why mainstream Bible believers can say "God" and be referring to the Father, the Son, or the Holy Spirit. It is because they are One in the same. The New Testament is filled with passages that state that God is Jesus (John 1:1 & 14, John 14:9, Col 1:16, Col 2:9, Phil 2:6) and that Jesus is God (John 10:30). So, while it is difficult to fully comprehend how Jesus can be on one hand God and on the other hand His Son, the fact remains true. To this day, I still have no real grasp on it, nor can I completely explain it to you now. I do, however, believe that the Bible is the written word of God and I can therefore trust its authority. Since He is smarter than I am in everything, I rely on His Word for clarification. If He says in His Book that Jesus is God and His Son, I am left with only one logical conclusion. I believe Him.

> Luke 5:20-26
> *And when he saw their faith, he said unto him, Man, thy sins are forgiven thee. And the scribes and the Pharisees began to reason, saying, Who is this which speaketh blasphemies? Who can forgive sins, but God alone? But when Jesus perceived their thoughts, he answering said unto them, What reason ye in your hearts? Whether is easier, to say, Thy sins be forgiven thee; or to say, Rise up and Walk? But that ye may know that the Son of man hath power upon earth to forgive sins, (he said unto the sick of the palsy,) I say unto thee, Arise, and take up thy couch, and go into thine house. And immediately he rose up before them, and took up that whereon he lay, and departed to his own house, glorifying God. And they were all amazed, and they glorified God, and were filled with fear, saying, We have seen strange things today.*

I like this passage because of the Pharisees' reaction to Jesus. These guys were the biblical scholars of their time and have a great point: Only God and God alone can truly forgive sins. Only the Creator of all has the complete wisdom to see each sin for what it is and the authority to either forgive or punish for it. For what is sin but an act against the One who created right and wrong in the first place?

Seeing their faith struggling, Jesus cuts straight to the point and says that He wants us all to know that He has the authority, that He is equal to God, and that He is God. This statement, which Jesus made several times throughout His ministry, was the reason people everywhere wanted Him dead. They heard Him boldly proclaim time after time that He was God and it angered them.

These Pharisees and Jews saw His declaration not as fact but as blasphemy, and they eventually killed Him for it. What the ancient Jews did not realize is that Jesus was perfect and would never lead anyone astray (Tit. 1:2). So when Jesus states that He has the power on earth to forgive sins, an act which only God can do, the only conclusion we can derive is that Jesus must be God. Jesus is who He says He is.

I had an interesting thought while I was studying the Ten Commandments a while back. I have read them several times throughout the years but on this day in particular, the first Commandment really stuck out to me. It reads *"Thou shalt have no other gods before me"* (Exod. 20:3). I then started to think of what Joseph Smith taught regarding the plurality of Gods. Remember, Mormons are textbook polytheists. They acknowledge that the Bible says that God the Father, Jesus, and the Holy Ghost are one but consistently claim this is only in purpose and not in a triune existence. As such, they believe in at least three different Gods. But God commands us not to have *any* other gods before Him. The very first commandment proclaims to the world that there is only one God, and that He alone deserves our worship. It is not difficult to see that by simply being polytheists Mormons have violated the very first commandment of God.

Furthermore, what the LDS church seems to be forgetting is that one of the primary reasons Jesus was crucified was because He claimed to not only be a God, but to be *the* God. He did not simply claim to have the same purpose as God, for if

He did the Hebrews would not have tried to kill him. Instead He made *"himself equal with God"* (John 5:18) and that was why the people sought to kill Him. Yet, even today the LDS church still holds to the "three separate Gods" theory despite this inconsistency.[6] In doing so, the LDS church has called into question the omniscience of God. For if God was all-knowing then why would He create a law – the first commandment – that would be undermined by the existence and teachings of His Son, Jesus? God is always consistent and wonderfully faultless. His laws have never and will never violate His existence. Since the Bible states there is only one God, that Jesus is God, and that Jesus is the Son of God, then we must conclude that the Father, the Son, and the Holy Spirit are One personage.

---

[6] *True to the Faith – A Gospel Reference*, "Godhead" (2004), 73-74

What is the Biblical View of Salvation?

Mormonism is a works-based religion. They believe that you are somewhat saved by Jesus' sacrifice, but if you want to enjoy the fullness of His joy in the highest degree then you must follow His teachings and perform essential church ordinances. You have to earn it. This, though, is contrary to God's plan. The Bible teaches that if anyone believes in Jesus as their personal Lord and Savior, He will be faithful to save them from their sins and grant them eternal life with Him (Rom. 10:9, 1 John 1:9, John 3:16). Furthermore, it states that there is nothing on earth that anyone can do to somehow earn salvation. Paul said that there are no "good" people and that we all fall short of God's standards (Rom. 3:9, 23). As such, we deserve eternal damnation. Thankfully, redemption is not something we can earn. The Bible says, *"for by grace are ye saved through faith, and that not of yourselves: it is the gift of God: Not of works, lest any man should boast."* (Eph. 2:8-9). There is nothing we can do to earn salvation because we are sinners. The only name by which we can be saved is Jesus (Acts 4:12).

"Knowing that a man is not justified by the works of the law, but by the faith of Jesus Christ, even we have believed in Jesus Christ, that we might be justified by the faith of Christ, and not by the works of the law: for by the works of the law shall no flesh be justified." (Gal. 2:16). Abiding by the rules, performing good works, and being a good person cannot get you into Heaven.

What the LDS church has done in recreating God's plan of salvation is strip some of the power out of the cross and placed that burden on their member's shoulders. The LDS Church says that you must do *something* in order to be saved. However, if there is *something* you can do to be saved then His Great White

Throne of Judgment (Rev 20:11-15) is nullified. God would no longer have final say in who gets into Heaven; we would. Furthermore, the blood of Jesus Christ would no longer be sufficient enough to save anyone right where they stand. While this does create a motivated congregation, it motivates them away from the true good news of the gospel. We already established that none of us are good, not even one (Rom. 3:10). If we are sinners, how can our impure works even compare to Christ's perfect life and His death on the cross? There is no comparison. Nothing we can do could ever grant us access into Heaven. We are fallen and, therefore, unholy. Therefore, even our best efforts are tainted (Isa. 64:6). What we need to realize is that if His blood is not sufficient to cleanse us from all unrighteousness then, in effect, we cannot fully trust in the blood of Christ for salvation. What a horrible thought! In Mormonism, Christ's sacrifice on the cross was not good enough, thus requiring works as a supplement to His wonderful gift.

Who are we though, but wretched sinners? Can the actions of a guilty inmate on death row earn him freedom? Of course not! His actions have already condemned him to die. Friends, realize that this is how we stand before God. There is nothing we can do to earn a seat at His table. This, though, is precisely the good news! It means you can absolutely trust the blood of Jesus to save you right where you are, without question! In fact, the Bible teaches that His blood is the only thing you can always rely on.

When we try to earn our salvation, the Bible says that instead of drawing nearer to God, we actually pull away and separate ourselves from Him (Gal 5:4). The only thing that counts is our relationship with Jesus (Gal 6:15). As a result, we should not even try to earn our way into His presence! God has done all the work and should receive all the credit and glory. He offers salvation as a free gift, and the only thing we need to "do" is accept it. What is so amazing is that our God is so wonderful and so loving that He offers it despite our constant rebellion and our short comings.

Let me put it this way. Imagine if someone gave you a birthday present, but told you that in order to receive it you had to wash their car. Would not the gift, by definition, cease to be a gift simply because you had to do something for it? Conversely, say you had given a close friend a very thoughtful and precious gift. Imagine that when you gave your friend their gift they immediately opened up their wallet and asked you how much you paid for it. Would you not be a little offended that they even entertained the thought of paying you back? You gave them the present out of the kindness of your heart and because you cared for them, not because you were expecting compensation. Would not that response eliminate your joy as the present giver? This is essentially what we do to God when we reach into our spiritual wallets and try to earn salvation.

Earlier I told an anecdote about a boy trying to purchase a bicycle in order to convey the idea of the Mormon plan of salvation. To contrast, I will present an analogy for the Biblical explanation of salvation. Instead of being eight years old, imagine you are nineteen years old and looking for a car for college. Upon hearing your desire your father agrees to take you to a dealership in a few months. You immediately start to save as much money as you can. However, college is expensive and you have no choice but to take out a couple of student loans. Right away, you are deeply in debt. In addition, you realize that you cannot neglect your other necessities, such as rent, food, and clothes. This means that any little money you do get from your minimum wage job is all but spoken for. And, being a typical kid, you eliminate the rest of your paycheck trying to maintain your social life and reputation. Cost after cost adds up and you cannot seem to make any headway towards the purchase of your car. So, you decide to get a couple of credit cards just to help ease the burden, which you quickly max out.

When the time comes to purchase your car you are not only broke, but are heavily in debt. Your father holds up his end of the deal and drives you to the dealership anyway. Your dream car is easily selected and before you know it the contract is all drawn up. The salesman runs your credit and tells you, to your embarrassment, that not only do you not have enough money to cover the car, but you do not even qualify for a loan. You start to cry because you realize that even though you tried your best to save all the money you could, all you could muster was thousands of dollars of debt. Thankfully, your father is an amazing, loving, and gracious dad. He says to you, "Child, do not worry. I love you and I will take care of this." He then tells the salesman to ring up the car under his name, and writes a check for the full amount. In addition to your car, your father has also been on the phone with all of your credit card and student loan companies and has completely wiped out all of your debt.

This is what our God has done for us. Our sins have placed us further and further into debt, despite our best efforts. Yet in His infinite love and wealth, He sent His Son to completely pay our debts and grant us eternal life. There is therefore nothing we can do or even need to do but rest comfortably in the pierced hands of our Savior.

Where is Jesus?

This then brings us to the point in which we can answer the title question: "Where is Jesus?" We first had to define who Jesus of the Bible was so that we would recognize Him when we sought after Him. After desperately trying to find the Biblical Jesus within the LDS doctrine and always coming up short, one can only conclude that the biblical Jesus just is not there. When the LDS church placed additional requirements for salvation and added clarifiers to the nature of Jesus Christ, the biblical Jesus was pushed out and the Mormon Jesus took over. This means that not only is the true Jesus over looked, but so is His message, power, and gifts. None of these things are able to be fully seen, learned, or enjoyed within the LDS church.

The Bible tells us that Jesus is the sole provider of salvation, yet in Mormonism He merely plays a supporting role to our efforts. Jesus said that He is God and one with the father, yet in Mormonism He is just the best version of you, me, the angels, and the demons. With these facts understood, we can only conclude that their Jesus and the Bible's Jesus are not the same person.

I have presented to many of my Mormon friends the dissimilarities between the Biblical Jesus and the Mormon Jesus several times. I have also stated that these differences are just a few of the reasons many do not view Mormons as Christian. The response I get whenever I bring this point up is often spoken in anger and frustration. "Our church has His name on it! How can we not be Christian?" Whenever I am faced with such an obviously sensitive issue, I have tried to let God respond from His Word:

Matthew 7:21-23

Not every one that saith unto me, Lord, Lord, shall enter into the kingdom of heaven; but he that doeth the will of my Father which is in heaven. Many will say to me in that day, Lord, Lord, have we not prophesied in thy name? and in thy name have cast out devils? and in thy name done many wonderful works? And then will I profess unto them, I never knew you: depart from me, ye that work iniquity.

Jesus Himself is telling us there are people that know His name but did not know Him personally. They will say to Him, "Jesus I know you! I told people about you! I went to a church with your name boldly written on its doors!" but they will be cast away from His presence. I believe the LDS church would fall under this category. Their name may be The Church of Jesus Christ of Latter Day Saints, and they may read the Bible, and they may claim to teach about Jesus, but it is just not the correct Jesus. They are simply using the same name for a different person altogether.

Section Two:
Pre-Mortal and Post-Mortal Existence

"As man now is, God once was; as God is now man may be."

-Lorenzo Snow
5th President of the Church of Jesus Christ of Latter Day Saints
The Teachings of Lorenzo Snow, ed. Clyde Williams [1984], 1.

The Before and Afterlife

Heaven is our final destination. It is a place where we can live with God in peace. There is no sorrow, no pain, no struggles, and no stress. It is paradise. For some, a superficial understanding of Heaven is sufficient. The simple fact that there is a Heaven and that they are going there someday is enough. However, I believe that a person's understanding and view of Heaven can actually influence how they live their life. Heaven is our prize. It is there where we will finally find rest from our troubles. Through the process of 'looking forward' our perceptions will change, as well as our attitudes, reactions, and priorities.

And though Heaven is what all believers look forward to, the architecture of the LDS Heaven is drastically different from that of other mainstream belief systems. For starters, the LDS doctrine teaches that all human beings existed in Heaven before their earthly birth. They also believe in a type of purgatory existence. Mormons believe that instead of one Heaven there are actually three and the requirements to get into each one is a bit different. Even Hell is a bit different than that of mainstream belief; partly because not every Mormon even believes it exists[7]. Lastly, Mormons teach that even the highest Heaven does not have to be the final destination.

In the next few chapters we will discuss each of these differences with the sole intention of maintaining our primary focus of seeking Jesus. As you read, I would also challenge you to ask yourself if having the LDS view of the afterlife alters your perception of Jesus and His placement in your life.

---

[7] Laidler, Brenton. "LDS Survey." 13 March 2014

In addition, I want the reader to know that in my research on this topic I have noticed that the afterlife is not discussed in great detail within the LDS church. Though only marginally explained, the LDS church's view on the afterlife is extremely complex. The specifics of the pre-mortal existence, Heaven, Hell, and beyond have so many components that it tends to illicit more questions than it actually answers. When I was still involved with the church these drastic differences led me to have a number of conversations with my friends and the LDS missionaries in an attempt to gain understanding. Unfortunately, the response I kept getting was, "that has yet to be revealed." I basically could never get a definitive answer. Confused, I began a more in-depth exploration in an attempt to better understand the Mormon pre and post mortal existence. Here is what I discovered.

Where Did I Come From?

As stated earlier, according to LDS doctrine we existed in Heaven before we lived on earth and we did so as spiritual offspring of God the Father. However, what I did not divulge is that in the LDS doctrine God the Father is actually married and His wife is often lovingly referred to as our Heavenly Mother. Given that Mormons believe in this heavenly family unit, our existence then as spiritual beings is not as created beings but rather spiritual babies born from propagation. "Latter-day Saints infer from authoritative sources of scripture and modern prophecy that there is a Heavenly Mother as well as a Heavenly Father...parenthood requires both father and mother, whether for the creation of spirits in the pre-mortal life or of physical tabernacles on earth. A heavenly mother shares parenthood with the Heavenly Father. This concept leads Latter-day Saints to believe that she is like him in glory, perfection, compassion, wisdom, and holiness."[8] Stated simply, God the Father and Heavenly Mother came together in a sexual manner and the entire human race was born and lived with God the Father in Heaven as spirits.

Even though we were in the highest Heaven with God – as that is the only Heaven God could exist in - we could not experience complete joy. According to Mormon beliefs, this can only come after one receives a physical body. Here is what the LDS church's magazine had to say in one of their articles about the body.

---

[8] Cannon, Elaine Anderson. Encyclopedia of Mormonism, "*Mother in Heaven*". New York: Macmillan, 1992

"One foundational gospel truth about the body is the principle that having a physical body is a godlike attribute-you are more like God with a body than without. Our religion stands virtually alone in believing that God has a tangible body of flesh and bone and that our bodies were literally created in His likeness...To become as God is requires gaining a body like He has and learning to correctly comprehend and use it. Those who chose not to follow God in the premortal state were denied mortal bodies. The Prophet Joseph Smith stated that Satan's lack of a body is punishment to him. The body then is necessary for progression and for obtaining a fullness of joy. Having a mortal body indicates that you chose righteously in the premortal state."[9]

Mormon doctrine teaches that we needed to come down to earth and receive a physical body in order to become more like Him. The reasoning behind this belief is that in order to become like Him we must first go through all the same experiences as He did. Furthermore, the LDS church is only one of the few religions that teach the doctrine of God the Father having a physical body (D&C 130:22). Coupled with the belief that after we are all resurrected, our bodies will be restored in perfect form (Alma 11:43), the need for a physical body within the Mormon Church is very apparent.

Growing up in the church, this is about as far as I remember learning. However, upon further study I found that being spiritual babies is only part of the pre-mortal existence. Mormons believe that we did not just reside in Heaven with God as tiny babies but instead were "reared to maturity in the eternal mansions of the Father, prior to coming upon the earth in a temporal [physical] body."[10] According to LDS doctrine, we did not just exist, we lived. We learned things, grew, and

[9] Spangler, Diane L. "The Body, a Sacred Gift." *Ensign Magazine*, July 2005.
[10] *Teachings of Presidents of the Church: Joseph F. Smith* (The Church of Jesus Christ of Latter-day Saints, 1998), 335

matured into the individuals we are today. We even discovered our potential. For instance, leaders of the LDS church were believed to be ordained by God in this developmental stage of their pre-mortal existence, which the LDS church credits the Bible for revealing. *"Before I formed thee in the belly I knew thee; and before thou camest forth out of the womb I sanctified thee, and I ordained thee a prophet unto the nations"* (Jer. 1:5).

Even the structure of our families was decided in this pre-mortal state. According to LDS teachings, from the vantage point of Heaven we were able to see different people and couples, and God allowed us to choose which family we wanted to be a part of. This doctrine actually became a topic of teasing in my family as we would look at one another and say something along the lines of, "Do not get mad at me. You chose to be here!"

Furthermore, some of us experienced love and found the one we were to marry. I remember being taught this doctrine as a child and even watching movies on the subject, one of them being the 1989 musical "Saturday's Warrior."

I should warn the reader that even though this doctrine is widely accepted, taught, and publicized, it is not LDS sanctioned doctrine. President Joseph F. Smith stated, there is "...no scriptural justification for the belief that we had the privilege of choosing our parents and our life companions in the spirit world. This belief has been advocated by some, and it is possible that in some instances it is true, but it would require too great a stretch of the imagination to believe it to be so in all, or even in the majority of cases."[11] Nevertheless, the belief in pre-mortal, premarital "choosing" has not been squelched and this idea is still very common today.

---

[11] Joseph Fielding Smith, *The Way to Perfection.* (Deseret Book Co, 1931), 44.

The Spirit World

Death is a fate that none of us will escape. It is like the old cliché says, "Nothing is certain but death and taxes."

Alma 40:11
Now, concerning the state of the soul between death and the resurrection – Behold, it has been made known unto me by an angel, that the spirits of all men, as soon as they are departed from this mortal body, yea, the spirits of all men, whether they be good or evil, are taken home to that God who gave them life.

The ancient LDS prophet Alma says that everybody will eventually be taken home[12] regardless of whether or not you are a good person or an evil person. Notice though that Alma also mentions a *"state of the soul"* in which we will exist between our death and the final resurrection. This state is often referred to within the LDS church as the spirit world. According to LDS doctrine, this spirit world is broken down into two realms: Spirit Prison and Spirit Paradise.

Spirit Prison is reserved for the evil doers, the wicked, and the unbelievers. It is a place where the people who have not received the gospel of Jesus Christ in this life must await their judgment. LDS scripture teaches:

Alma 40:13-14
And then shall it come to pass, that the spirits of the wicked, yea, who are evil – for behold, they have no part

---

[12] *Book of Mormon Student Manual*, 2009. 242-47

*nor portion of the Spirit of the Lord; for behold, they
chose evil works rather than good; therefore the spirit of
the devil did enter into them, and take possession of their
house – and these shall be cast out into outer darkness;
there shall be weeping, and wailing, and gnashing of
teeth, and this because of their own iniquity, being led
captive by the will of the devil. Now this is the state of
the souls of the wicked, yea, in darkness, and a state of
awful, fearful looking for the fiery indignation of the
wrath of God upon them; thus they remain in this state,
as well as the righteous in paradise, until the time of
their resurrection.*

In Spirit Prison the inhabitants will find themselves in a
great deal of suffering. LDS scripture says there will be
"weeping, and wailing, and gnashing of teeth," very similar to
the Biblical view of the pain and torment people will experience
in Hell (Matt. 8:12, Matt. 13:42, Luke 13:28). Unlike Hell, this
state of existence is only temporary. Remember that Spirit
Prison is a stage between death and the resurrection. This
means that after the Second Coming, the Spirit Prison will no
longer be needed. This stage is just a supernatural holding cell
until judgment day.

Another reason that Spirit Prison is only temporary is
because it is a stage of purification, whereby one could be
permitted to leave. According to Mormon doctrine, Joseph F.
Smith, the sixth prophet of the Church of Jesus Christ of Latter
Day saints, was given a vision regarding the Spirit Prison. He
acknowledged that during the time between the crucifixion and
His resurrection, Jesus organized messengers. These
messengers were given His power and authority to carry a light
to these imprisoned souls (D&C 138:27-30). Mormon Doctrine
teaches that these prisoners still have the opportunity to follow
Jesus and escape this temporary Hell. All that is required of
them is to accept His message. The truly repentant will have
the doors of their prisons unlocked and be able to "dwell with the

righteous in paradise."[13] Those that still choose to reject Jesus' message will remain in prison until the resurrection.

Spirit Paradise, on the other hand is a place where the righteous and faithful await their resurrection in splendor and glory. In this state, the righteous will experience "*happiness...a state of rest, a state of peace, where they shall rest from all their troubles and from all care, and sorrow.*" (Alma 40:12). When Jesus was in this state He preached to all the souls living there and "*gave them power to come forth, after his resurrection from the dead, to enter into his Father's kingdom, there to be crowned with immortality and eternal life, and continue thenceforth their labor as had been promised by the Lord, and be partakers of all blessings which were held in reserve for them that love him*" (D&C 138:51-52).

This state is drastically different than that of Spirit Prison. It almost seems to be a sort of 'preview of what is to come' for the righteous. These righteous men and women not only reside in peace with other believers but I would venture to guess that they are reassured with their life choices and are able to rest easy knowing that they have done well in the eyes of the Lord.

---

[13] Parsons, Robert J. Encyclopedia of Mormonism, "*Spirit Prison*". New York: Macmillan, 1992

Three Heavens
and a Hell

Whichever state you resided in after your earthly death, when the time comes we will all stand before God and be judged (Rev 20:11-12). Mormons believe that after God's judgment it will be revealed to us which Heaven we are to spend eternity. The second prophet of the church, Brigham Young, revealed that in fact "all men...will be saved in some kingdom."[14]

There are three kingdoms in which we can inherit. From least to greatest, they are the Telestial, the Terrestrial, and the Celestial. Mormons further claim that this doctrine, while predominately found in LDS scriptures, can also be found in the Bible. They quote the apostle Paul when he tells the church in Corinth "*I know a man in Christ above fourteen years ago, (whether in the body, I cannot tell; or whether out of the body, I cannot tell: God knoweth;) such an one caught up to the third heaven*" (2 Cor. 12:2).

These three kingdoms of Mormon Heaven vary in degrees of glory, or splendor. Often times the LDS church will compare them with the brightness of our sun, moon, and stars, to help explain their varying magnificence. Our sun, for instance, is used as a symbol for the highest degree of Heaven while the moon and stars are used to refer to the middle and least kingdoms of Heaven, respectively. This symbolism is helpful in explaining how greater the reward is in the Celestial Kingdom than say the Telestial Kingdom, as the brightness of the sun is much more brilliant than that of the stars. In addition, they use an excerpt of the Apostle Paul's letter to the churches in Corinth (1 Cor. 15:39-41) to validate using this comparison.

---

[14] Young, Brigham, "Personality of God-His Attributes-Eternal Life, Etc." in *Journal of Discourse*, Vol. 11, Discourse 19, (George D. Watt, 1854-1886).

The Telestial Kingdom, the glory of the stars, is the lowest out of all the kingdoms of Heaven. Though it may be the least of the three, it is still a wonderful place to be. LDS scripture states that the beauty of this kingdom "*surpasses all understanding*" (D&C 76:89) and "is far better than this world we now know."[15] This kingdom then is better than our best days on earth and even more beautiful. In fact, I remember being taught that the Telestial kingdom is basically a perfected earth. Moreover, "The Prophet Joseph Smith told us that if we could get one little glimpse into the Telestial glory even, the glory is so great that we would be tempted to commit suicide to get there."[16]

With a kingdom so rich in splendor, one would think that only the righteous would obtain it. That is not the case. Remember those people who rejected Jesus' message in the Spirit Prison? They are the ones who will inherit the Telestial Kingdom. LDS doctrine teaches that this degree of Heaven is reserved for those who have rejected the gospel of Jesus Christ, are unrepentant for their sins but, have not committed the unpardonable sin of denying the Holy Spirit. These people are those that have been "*thrust down to hell. These are they who shall not be redeemed from the devil until the last resurrection...*" (D&C 76:84-85a). So, even though these people have absolutely rejected the gospel of Jesus Christ, they will absolutely be saved from everlasting torment.

The next kingdom is referred to as the Terrestrial kingdom, equated to the brightness of the moon. Since it is the second kingdom, its splendor must be greater than that of the third. As such, we can rightly assume that the Terrestrial kingdom is exponentially greater than the Telestial in every aspect.

LDS scripture states that that the inhabitants of this kingdom are those "*who died without law. ... Who received not*

---

[15] John A. Widtsoe, *Evidences and Reconciliations* (Bookcraft, 1943), 199.
[16] Eldred G. Smith, March 10, 1964, BYU Speeches of the Year, 1964, p.4

the testimony of Jesus in the flesh, but afterwards received it. These are they who are honorable men of the earth, who were blinded by the craftiness of men. These are they who receive of his glory, but not of his fullness. These are they who receive of the presence of the Son, but not of the Father. ... These are they who are not valiant in the testimony of Jesus; wherefore, they obtain not the crown over the kingdom of our God" (D&C 76:72b-77, 79). Mormons believe that these people were *"honorable"* members of society but were simply blinded by the things of this world. Since they died as non-believers, or *"without law,"* they were cast into Spirit Prison. However, while in their imprisoned state, they were visited by His messengers and accepted His gospel. They were then granted freedom from their prison and taken to Spiritual Paradise. After His Second Coming and the resurrection, these men and women will be taken to the Terrestrial Kingdom where they will receive a degree of God's glory, though not the fullness of it (v. 76). LDS scriptures also state that they will be in the presence of Jesus, but not God the Father (v. 77). So while this Kingdom is magnificently better than the previous one, it is not the best place one can spend eternity.

The highest degree of glory is found in the Celestial Kingdom. Its brilliance and glory is compared with the brightness of the sun. Those who have lived a Godly life, who have lived according to His word and commandments, who were faithful until the end are able to live forever in the presence of God the Father and Jesus Christ (who appears to have the ability to travel between, at least, the top two kingdoms). These people have received the gospel of Jesus Christ, believed on his name, were baptized, kept the commandments, received the Holy Spirit by laying on of hands by an ordained priesthood holder, and were sealed (see "Section 3 - Can Marriage Be Eternal") to Him in the temple, ordained as priests in the order of Melchizedek, and who are members of His church (D&C 76:50-57). This kingdom also includes the righteous men and women who passed away before Joseph Smith revealed his revelation. *"All who have died without a knowledge of this gospel, who would have received it if they had been permitted to tarry, shall be heirs of the celestial kingdom of God"* (D&C 137:7). Lastly, children who have not reached the age of accountability are also allowed to enter into the Celestial kingdom (D&C 137:10).

In addition to being the greatest of all the Heavens, the Celestial Kingdom is where one can continue their progress towards exaltation. Here, they continue to progress, learn, and grow, and then, hopefully, receive the opportunity to become like God the father. I will talk more on this subject in the next chapter, which is entitled "The Mormon Meaning of Life."

The final home where people can eternally reside after the resurrection is not a Heaven at all. Mormons do not refer to this place as Hell, but rather Outer Darkness. This "realm," for lack of a better term, is Satan's lair. It is only for three types of creatures: The Devil himself, his fallen angels, and the sons of perdition, *"of whom I say that it had been better for them never to have been born; For they are vessels of wrath, doomed to suffer the wrath of God, with the devil and his angels in eternity; Concerning whom I have said there is no forgiveness in this world nor in the world to come"* (D&C 76:32-34). These men and women were once believers but later denied the Holy Spirit and Jesus Christ. I have been told by some that these "sons of perdition" might only refer to those people who have been baptized in the LDS church and were given the LDS priesthood but then renounced that faith and proceeded to persecute the Mormon Church.

The Mormon
Meaning of Life

I quoted Lorenzo Snow at the start of this section as saying "As man now is God once was; as God is now man may be." We have already seen some of the doctrine behind the first part of this sentence, which says that God was as we are now. Mormon doctrine does not shy away from the fact that they are one of the few religions that teach that God has a body and was once a man. He is now fully progressed and has achieved His 'God' status. The idea that someone can achieve a 'God' status is what the second part of the sentence refers to. It is what Mormons believe to be our eternal goal: To achieve exaltation and become a God.

"The Church of Jesus Christ of Latter-day Saints, basing its belief on divine revelation, ancient and modern, proclaims man to be the direct and lineal offspring of Deity. God Himself is an exalted man, perfect, enthroned, and supreme."[17] While the particulars of which "earth" God existed in are a bit confusing, the doctrine of His humanity is very clear. The LDS church teaches that God was just like you and me and was a man of flesh and bones. By assumption then we can conclude that, like us, He also sinned, felt shame and hurt, and eventually died. However, since God was a righteous man, He earned a place in the Celestial Kingdom, where He progressed until He became God the Father. Mormons believe that He now experiences an eternal joy and it is out of His love for us that He offers us a similar path.

The LDS church quotes Bible verses to support this claim, saying that "...*ye might be filled with all the fullness of God*" (Eph. 3:19b) and "*To him that overcometh will I grant to sit*

---

[17] The First Presidency of the Church, "The Origin of Man." *Ensign Magazine*, February 2002

with me in my throne..." (Rev 3:21a) are references to us having the potential for exaltation. They claim that since the Bible tells us that we shall be like Him (1 John 3:2) we therefore will have the opportunity to become a God, just as He did. The passage that I have heard quoted most by Mormons in regards to exaltation is from one of Jesus' sermons. While He was preaching to the multitudes, Jesus said, *"Be ye therefore perfect, even as your Father which is in heaven is perfect"* (Mat 5:48). Mormons believe that striving to be like Him is a commandment from God. They believe that Jesus is alluding to the fact that it is possible to achieve God's level of perfection, thus creating the idea that becoming a God is also achievable. It is further explained that in order to be perfect, one must perform all of the ordinances of the LDS church. The most important of these being receiving a Temple Endowment, or special spiritual blessings[18], and being married in the temple (D&C 131:1-4).

With all of that being said do not confuse the idea that everyone has the ability to become God with the notion that everyone will become a God. Mormons view each of us as having only the potential to become a god. It is not guaranteed even if they make it to the Celestial Kingdom that they will progress. There is still much more work to be done in order to achieve the fullness of glory.

The LDS church also makes the point that becoming a god in no way makes them somehow equal with God, or no longer under His rule. "We absolutely do not believe that we will ever be independent of God or no longer subject to Him. He will always be our God. We do not believe that we will take away His glory, but we only add to it by following Christ."[19]

The purpose then for this life, according to the LDS church, is pretty laid out. God wants us to be like Him. If this is true, then that should be our main focus. Everything we do and

---

[18] "Endowment," LDS Topics. www.lds.org/topics/endowment
[19] Fordham, Michael W. "Do We Have the Potential to become Like God?" FairMormon. 1997-2014. http://en.fairmormon.org/perspectives/publications/do-we-have-the-potential-to-become-like-god

say should be a reflection of that God-ship mindset. As earthly beings, Mormons believe that we need to follow all of the requirements God put in place so that we may be admitted into the Celestial Kingdom. Once there, it is believed that God will have more for us to do and learn in order to help us achieve our ultimate goal. And, hopefully, someday we will have the unique opportunity to become the elite of the elite and through God's love and provision, honor Him by becoming a god ourselves.

What Does the Bible
Say About All This?

In regards to the pre-mortal existence, the LDS church has adopted a unique viewpoint. They stand firm in claiming that there is a Heavenly Mother. They declare that God and His wife came together to produce every human being that has ever lived. They further testify that we also lived with God and Mom in a pre-mortal state where we grew, were given a path in life, and chose our families.

While very creative and convincing, this pre-mortal existence is simply not biblical. There is no Heavenly Mother. God alone sits enthroned in Heaven and rules over the entire earth (2 Kings 19:15). While the Bible does state that we are His children (Mat 5:45) it is not in the procreated sense. Paul tells us that it is when we become believers that we are adopted into His family and are called His children (Rom 8:15). As such, we are not the product of a Heavenly birth. God is our creator, and we become a new creation in Him when we become His disciple (2 Cor. 5:17). Biblically speaking, there are only two births we as humans can experience: one is from an earthly mother and the other is a spiritual birth, or being born again in Christ (John 3:1-7).

As a practicing Mormon, one of the most difficult things to wrap my head around was the idea that I was able to choose to be part of a family on earth while in the pre-mortal state. Since I am a product of a broken home, the notion that I would chose to be in a family with so many difficulties was very difficult to grasp. Many times I would say to myself, "What was I thinking when I chose to be a part of this family?" I then started to think why anyone would choose to be in anything but a privileged home. Why would anyone want to be in a family in a third world country? Why would anyone choose to be in a non-white American family in the 1960s? I wondered why anyone would choose to pick a family with a history of physical abuse, drug dependency, alcoholism, rape, incest, or crime.

The truth is we do not get to pick. Instead, our family structure was skillfully and intentionally designed and constructed. God strategically created and placed us in each of our families for His glory. As Jeremiah said, God knows all things and knew us before the formations of the world. This does not mean that He walked and talked with us before our time on earth. It means that God knew that He was going to create you exactly when He did and place you exactly where you are so that you would be able to do exactly what He has planned for you. How? Because God knows everything!

Mormons have also claimed that after we die we will await Jesus' second coming in the Spirit World. The righteous will enjoy a state of joy, peace, and rest in Paradise whereas the unrighteous will be confined to a fiery torment in Prison unless they accept His message. They further claim that the Spirit World is a person's last chance for salvation.

Now, some Mormons may claim that God instituted this "last chance" stage as a demonstration of His ever abundant grace. They would state that God loves us so much that He gives us one more chance to make the right decision and follow Him. To that, I would argue that the Bible teaches the exact opposite. His grace is only offered to us right up until we take our last breath. The Bible says we do not know what will happen tomorrow and should, therefore, not wait to do what God asks of us (James 4:14-17). The writer of Hebrews tells us that we must believe in God the day we *"hear his voice"* (Heb. 3:15). Not tomorrow, not when it is convenient, not after we pass away, but *"today."* This means there are no second chances. This life is our last chance. That is why the Bible urges us not to wait to choose to follow Him (Proverbs 27:1). Procrastination is dangerous and God warns us not to be ensnared by laziness, especially when it comes to faith in Christ. *"The soul of the sluggard desireth, and hath nothing: but the soul of the diligent shall be made fat"* (Prob. 13:4).[20]

In the Gospel of Luke, Jesus tells the story of the rich man and a beggar named Lazarus. The rich man enjoyed a life of plenty while Lazarus was always hungry and his body was full of sores. When they both died, Lazarus was taken up to Heaven and the rich man was taken down to Hell. While in torment, the rich man cried out, "*I pray thee therefore, father, that thou wouldest send [Lazarus] to my father's house: For I have five brethren; that he may testify unto them, lest they also come into this place of torment*" (Luke 16:27-28). Two things come to mind when reading this. First off, Jesus does not mention that this rich man went to Spirit Prison. He says that when he died he went immediately to Hell. Secondly, if the rich man knew of a way to escape his torment, would not he have asked for it? Instead, he pleads with Abraham to save his family from the same fate. The rich man understood that he was out of chances, but his family still could still be saved. But "*Abraham saith unto him, They have Moses and the prophets; let them hear them*" (Luke 16:29). Abraham tells him that God has already made His message abundantly clear through his prophets and the scriptures. If they do not accept it in this life, their fate will be the same as his. The rich man learned the hard way that this life is our only chance to accept Jesus as Lord and Savior.

Furthermore, Jesus made a big deal out of the fact that we are called to go and preach unto the ends of the earth (Mark 16:15). We as believers have a responsibility to share His good news before it is too late. If Mormonism is right, then it will never be too late, for after they die they will still hear the good news but just in a not so pleasant setting. In reality, this life is our first and only chance to come to know the true and living God. Do not wait!

---

[20] S. Michael Houdmann, "What does the Bible say about procrastination?" www.gotquestions.org, (June 10, 2014)

With purgatory out of the way, Heaven and Hell become the next topic of discussion. Again, the LDS church has a unique claim that there are multiple degrees of glory. But are there really three Heavens? Did Paul truly see his friend being lifted into the Celestial kingdom?

First, let me address the topic of the Apostle Paul's mention of a third heaven. One must understand that the way the ancient apostles spoke is much different than that of our current vernacular. The ancient Hebrews used the word 'heaven' to describe not just where God lives, but also the sky, the clouds, and the universe. Each of these Hebrew heavens had a level, with the highest heaven depicting where God lives. In this case, the first heaven would most likely refer to the sky, the second to outer space, and the third to God's home. In other words, if Paul were an apostle today, he would simply have said that he saw his friend being taken up into Heaven to live with God.

Biblically speaking, Heaven is a place where we as believers of Jesus Christ can live for all eternity in His presence. There will be no suffering, no pain, no sin, and no problems. All you need to do is believe in His name and He will save you. Take for instance the thief on the cross. He lived a life apart from God, yet in his last moments, He cried out to God and Jesus saved him (Luke 23:32-43). Faith in Jesus grants us a spot in the everlasting presence of our Father. There we will enjoy a peace that knows no bounds.

It is at this point in several of my discussions that a lot of Mormons have asked me if I thought it was fair that this thief enjoys the same glory as someone who devotes their entire life to God, thereby implying the need for three distinct heavens. I always try to respond by pointing them to the Bible. In Matthew, Jesus tells the parable of the workers in the vineyard (Matt. 20:1-16). To paraphrase, the owner needs workers for his field and goes out every couple of hours to hire more workers. At the end of the day He pays all of these workers, regardless of how long they worked, the same amount. This angers the people who were hired at the beginning of the day because they feel since they worked longer hours they should be paid more. *"But he answered one of them, and said, Friend, I do thee no wrong: didst thou agree with me for a penny? Take that thine is, and go thy way: I will give unto this last, even as unto thee. Is it not lawful for me to do what I will with mine own? Is thine eye evil, because I am good?"* (Matt. 20:13-15). I believe this parable touches upon this very topic. Mormonism, being a works based religion, looks at the amount of "work" and associates that to a degree of glory. Jesus teaches us, in this parable, that this is not the case. Our glory is the same across the board, regardless of how long or how hard you "worked". Like it or not, this parable teaches that God grants every believer a seat in His Kingdom regardless of how long they have believed and served.

Some might say then that getting into Heaven is too easy. "So all I have to do is believe? That's it? It seems too simple." In a way, they are absolutely right, and praise God for it! God does all the work for us and therefore deserves all the credit. Jesus meets us where we are not where we should be. He loves us so much that He made returning to him as simple as A, B, C. We admit that we are sinners in need of a savior, we believe that Jesus is God's son who died for our sins, and we simply choose every day to follow Him. Trust me, the Christian life is not easy, but the choice to become one is.

Additionally, if one would stop and think about the different degrees of glory Mormonism teaches, they would find that only a small, minute amount of people will ever experience Outer Darkness. This means that the majority of people will be saved. I remember coming to this conclusion as a Mormon and it made me wonder. If Heaven is a reward for basically everyone then what is the point of this life? Heaven, or at least the lowest degree of Heaven, would be filled with the unrepentant non-believers who wanted nothing to do with a God. These people, who purposely and consistently rejected God and His salvation, are still saved from an eternity of destruction. It would seem that despite all of their sin and rebellion they are still granted an eternity of bliss. To me, this does not seem right. What is the point then of repentance, of faith, the Bible, or even Jesus? If rejecting God has no real consequence, then following God has no real reward. Where is the pull to preach the gospel to the ends of the earth (Matt. 24:14)? Furthermore, logically speaking, it might actually be more beneficial to mankind if the Gospel was never spread at all. For in Mormonism, you cannot be condemned to Hell for denying a religion you have never been introduced to.

This brings us to the topic of Hell, Heaven's polar opposite. According to the Bible, those who have not accepted the free gift of salvation will still know who Jesus is and call Him Lord (Isaiah 45:23) but will be cast into the fiery torment (Mat. 13:41-42). These non-believers will live for all eternity away from His presence (2 Thes. 1:9). Since God is full of love, grace, peace, and joy, being removed from His presence is to experience the contrary. Pain, sorrow, torment, and destruction (Matt. 13:50, Jude 1:7) await all who do not choose to follow Christ. Satan and his demons will be there among the crowd since they were the first to reject God's authority. Hell is real, it is eternal, and it is horrible. Friends, heed the Bible's warnings and turn your lives to Christ.

Lastly, what does the Bible teach about the nature of God? Was God as we are now? Is God an exalted man? John 4:24 says that *"God is spirit, and they that worship him must worship him in spirit and in truth."* Jesus says that God is a spirit, or that He is spirit. Furthermore, when Jesus is resurrected and shows himself to the apostles, He tells them to look at His hands and His feet, to touch and feel how real He is, *"for a spirit hath not flesh and bones, as ye see me have"* (Luke 24:39). So, Jesus, who knows all things, says that spirits do not have flesh and bones. God the Father then is telling us, through His son, that He the Father is neither a man nor was He ever one.

Moreover, Jesus does command us to be perfect, but not so that we can become an all-powerful God ourselves. Far from it! Jesus was simply telling His followers to always strive to live a more righteous life. Jesus wanted people to throw down their sinful ways and follow Him. *"For by one sacrifice he has made perfect forever those who are being made holy"* (Heb. 10:14). All those who follow Jesus have already been made perfect by His blood. It was never God's intention to allude to the idea of Godship. He was merely urging His people to be perfected by His atonement and find themselves under the umbrella of His grace.

Furthermore, men are mortal, created, sinful beings. If God was just like us, as Mormons believe, then He was also mortal, created, and a sinner. This means that LDS members, in essence, worship a redeemed sinner. Now, I want the reader to really stop and think about the implications that this entails. I want to draw your attention to what Aaron Shafovaloff, a Christian apologist, wrote on the idea that God was once a sinner.

> "If our Heavenly Father (or any Heavenly Father in ultimate reality) was once perhaps a sinner, only sins which permanently disqualify or disable a person from achieving full Celestial exaltation unto godhood are sins that he absolutely never committed. Or to put it another way, any sin that doesn't permanently disqualify or disable a person from achieving full Celestial exaltation unto godhood is a sin that a Heavenly Father in Mormonism may have committed. The only sins which traditional Mormonism says permanently disqualify or disable a person from achieving godhood are murder (some Mormons even limit this to post-temple-covenant murder) and blasphemy against the Holy Ghost.
>
> Think about it. What are some sins that you find especially gross and heinous that a person can repent over unto Celestial exaltation and godhood? Those are

the sins that God of Mormonism may have committed, and those are sins that other Gods (either in the past ancestry of the Gods or the future lineage of Gods) may have committed."[21]

If Mormonism is correct, then the God we praise, worship and honor as being Holy, Holy, Holy is possibly guilty of any number of sins. Is this the God we worship? Was God ever a sinner? Does this accurately describe the Most High God, the King of Kings, the Lord of Lords, and the Great I am? Of course not! God was and always will be completely worthy of our praise. He is perfect, sinless, and one hundred percent pure.

Looking past the implied sinful nature of our God, we still run into the fact that our God was forgiven, redeemed, and exalted. But who redeemed him? It would have to be by someone who is greater than he is. This means that there would have to be some type of Jesus-being who saved our God in His sins. But then, should not our worship go to this savior instead since he would be greater? But then, where did that God come from? Was He too a sinner saved? Carrying out this logic then would only create an infinite and confusing timeline. Where would it end?

Thankfully, we can rest assured that our God has never sinned. He is perfect in every sense of the word, has always been without blemish, and has always been worthy of our praise. The fact that we worship God as being Holy, Holy, Holy (Isa. 6:3) testifies of this fact.

Everything has a beginning except for God (Gen. 1). The Bible tells us that God is eternal (Deut. 33:27, Rev 1:8). Though hard to understand, that is who He says He is. He proclaims to the world "I AM!" Not "I was," or "I started," but simply "I am".

---

[21] Aaron Shafovaloff, "What kind of sins did a Mormon god once perhaps commit?" www.godneversinned.com, (October, 29 2014)

God does not have a beginning or an end, which is part of His awesomeness and why we worship Him. He is so much more than we can even comprehend and we glorify His name because of it!

Finally, the LDS doctrine poses the idea that it is possible for us to become a God. The Bible tells us that this just is not so. The prophet Isaiah spoke on this very matter.

Isaiah 43:10
Ye are my witnesses, saith the Lord, and my servant whom I have chosen: that ye may know and believe me, and understand that I am he: before me there was no God formed, neither shall there be after me.

No one is going to become a god. That honor is solely reserved for the almighty Himself. The doctrine that the LDS church is promoting is completely contrary to the Bible. God is perfect, we are not. He was never like us. God is superior to us in every way possible. We can never be like Him nor even hope to be. Again, this is not bad news for it frees us up to understand our true purpose in this life. We are to honor and glorify God and share the light of Christ with everyone and anyone so that they can hear about the free gift of salvation offered by Jesus Christ, and be saved.

Where is Jesus?

To most Bible believers the idea of Heaven is a simple one: Experience eternal joy and peace in the arms of our Savior. That is it. Christians do not see Heaven as a stepping stone to something greater; they see it as the ultimate prize. Christ is our Savior and He is the focus, even after we have stopped breathing. His love is what saves us in the depths of our sin and, as a result of His free gift of salvation, it is our duty to bestow eternal honor and glory back on Him. Forever will we cast our crowns at His feet and will bask in His glory (Rev 4:10-11). What more could anyone ask for?

Paul tells the church in Philippi that *"the most important thing is that in every way...Christ is preached"* (Phil. 1:18 NIV). The LDS church has presented the world with an incredible view of the afterlife. It is not hard to see, however, that in Mormonism Jesus is not being preached. He is not the focal point; we are. It is safe to say that the ultimate goal in Mormonism is to be the best you can be so that you can enter into the Celestial kingdom where you can progress and hopefully become a god someday. This, though, is textbook idolatry. The Bible warns that *"No man can serve two masters"* (Matt. 6:24) and by making exaltation their end focus, the LDS church has created an idol above the person of Jesus. Mormons have stopped serving Christ and instead serve their own selfish desires. Jesus has been stripped of His deserving title of Savior and has been downgraded into a mere stepping stone towards the greater goal of God-ship. Friends, anytime you remove Jesus from his rightful place in receiving all glory, honor, and praise you disgrace His work on the cross. Jesus is the only One who deserves our attention, worship, and honor (Exod. 20:4-5).

I have spoken similar words to various friends and families throughout the years. Their responses always puzzle me. After hearing that my goal is just to live in Heaven and praise God forever and ever, they reply, "That's it? It sounds incredibly boring." They then ask why God gave them goals, aspirations, desires, a mind, and a heart that strives for perfection if not to eternally strive to be like Him! Friends, do you not see how perverse this type of thinking is to the gospel of Jesus Christ?

We are not the main focus of the Bible; God is. The Bible says that we are but lost, sinful, and condemned creations. It states that our actions are deserving of Hell. In literary terms, we, as human beings, are the damsels in distress. Since when is the damsel ever the main focus of the book? On the contrary, the focus is always on the hero. In the case of the Bible, our hero is God. Our hero is Jesus. The Bible says that our Hero stepped into our mess, became sin, died on a cross and rose again so that we no longer have to receive what we so rightly deserve. Since Jesus is the sole focus of the Bible, He should be the sole focus of our lives as well. Should our eternal destination be any different? Of course not!

Heaven is a wonderful, amazing place and I truly hope that I will one day see you there. But not as another created being striving for God-ship, but as a fellow believer worshiping our God for His wonderful grace displayed through the person of Jesus Christ.

Section Three:
Can Marriage Be Eternal

"Marriage is the foundry for social order, the fountain of virtue, and the foundation for eternal exaltation. Marriage has been divinely designated as an eternal and everlasting covenant. Marriage is sanctified when it is cherished and honored in holiness. That union is not merely between husband and wife; it embraces a partnership with God."

-Russell M. Nelson
Apostle of the Church of Jesus Christ of Latter-day Saints
Nurturing Marriage, Ensign, may 2006, p. 36

Wedding Bells Ringing

Mormons believe that marriage is very important. I cannot stress that enough. They see it as a direct call from God. Gordon B. Hinckley, a former prophet of the LDS church, stated, "The family is ordained of God. Marriage between man and woman is essential to His eternal plan."[22] According to the LDS faith, God has designed all of us to be married. They believe that His plan for us rides on the hopes of us finding that special someone to spend the rest of our lives with. It "is perhaps the most vital of all decisions and has the most far-reaching effects, for it has to do not only with immediate happiness, but also with eternal joys. It affects not only the two people involved, but also their families, particularly their children and their children's children, down through the latest generations."[23]

To be honest, this belief may not strike anyone as odd or necessarily wrong. Marriage and family are common themes that we see pop up time and time again. From movies to discounts at stores, the family unit plays a huge role in our culture. What may be news to you, though, is that the Mormon version of marriage and the family are actually quite different than what you may be used to.

When most people think of marriage, they think of a civil union between a man and a woman. This union goes until, as most ministers will say, "death do you part." This is not the type of marriage that is sought after in the Mormon Church. Instead, Mormons have taken it one step further and developed a way for man and woman to be together for all eternity. This is accomplished by not only being in a government recognized

---

[22] Hinckley, Gordon B. "The Family: A Proclamation to the World" September 23, 1995.
[23] Kimball, Spencer W. "The Importance of Celestial Marriage" October 22, 1976

union, but by performing that union in an LDS Temple and being sealed together for all eternity, as we will now discuss.

A Marriage That Even
Death Cannot Destroy

In the LDS faith, a man and a woman are sealed together in a Mormon temple with a bond that not even God will break. Sealing is the "generic term, [which] means the securing, determining, or establishing of a bond of legitimacy. Among members of the [LDS] church sealing refers to the marriage of a husband and wife and the joining together of children and parents in relationships that are to endure forever... [which is] referred to as "eternal marriage" or "celestial marriage""[24] Death then is only a temporary lapse in togetherness. It no longer has a stronghold on the family bond. For when both husband and wife are in Heaven, they will yet again experience wedded bliss, only this time it is in a perfect setting for all eternity.

In the Old Testament there were requirements to be able to gain access to the inner sanctuary of the Temple in Jerusalem, like being a descendant of Levi for instance. Similarly, there are several requirements for someone to be able to gain entry into an LDS temple to get married. A person cannot just request a temple marriage and be given one. Both the man and woman must be deemed worthy in order to gain entry into a Mormon Temple by having a temple recommend. The recommend is a card that is given out after an in depth interview with a church leader, typically a Ward bishop, who deems you worthy. They ask you questions regarding your faith, your dealings with your fellowmen, whether or not you sustain,

---

[24] Hyer, Paul V. Encyclopedia of Mormonism, "*Sealing: Temple Sealings*". New York: Macmillan, 1992

or support, the LDS church's leaders, and whether or not you are a full-tithe payer.[25]

"Then they visit a temple and receive initiatory ordinances and the blessing referred to as the temple Endowment. This entails the receipt of instruction and being put under covenant to obey eternal laws set forth by God, which if observed, will ensure a superior standard of morality, marriage and family life."[26] During the endowment ceremony, many covenants are made between the LDS members and God. This is also where LDS members receive their temple garments, or Mormon underwear.

It is only when a future bride and groom have acquired a temple recommend, received their endowments, and had a church official deem them worthy members of the LDS church, that they will be allowed a temple wedding. Once the ceremony is performed couples may rest easy knowing that no matter what life throws at them they will always be with their true love. The phrase "Until death do you part" no longer applies. Moreover, it also means that any children born to this newly married couple will also fully enjoy the bond of eternal togetherness. This is where the common Mormon motto "families can be together forever" comes into play.

---

[25] *"Temple Recommend Questions"* www.lds4u.com/lesson5/templequestions.htm (accessed 26 June 2014).
[26] Hyer, Paul V.

Do You Say I Do?

In addition to never having to worry about being separated from your family, a temple marriage provides you fulfillment in the LDS faith. *"In the celestial glory there are three heavens or degrees; And in order to obtain the highest, a man must enter into this order of the priesthood [meaning the new and everlasting covenant of marriage]; And if he does not, he cannot obtain it."* (D&C 131:1-3). The LDS church is very clear on this point: If you are unmarried, then you cannot become a God.

Growing up LDS, I was privy to a lot of behind the scenes interactions that most investigators would never see. Again, this is only my perception and I cannot say this happens in every church across the globe. I can, however, say it absolutely happened in all of mine. Young men were sent on their mission right after high school and told to be completely devoted to God. Back home, young women were being taught how valuable marriage is and that marrying a returned missionary is the best way to go. These young men then return homesick and longing for female companionship. Lucky for them they are greeted by these now primed young women ready to be married. It does not take long until these young men and women end up tying the knot. This whole 'rush to the altar' seemed completely normal to me at the time. As far as I could tell, these men and women were old enough to make their own decisions and their parents seemed pleased with the idea.

"Latter-day Saints...tend to marry early. 45% of LDS women and 23% of LDS men have married by age nineteen. By age twenty-one 74% of LDS women and 49% of LDS men have married. This is considerably higher than for any other religious group."[27]   There is a church-wide push for young men and women to be married. This is why a lot of Mormons get married at a younger age than most other people, in general. I believe this incentive derives from the fact that LDS doctrine states that in order to be a good, upstanding Mormon, one must be married.

President Spencer W. Kimball, in his speech at the Salt Lake Institute of Religion and at Ricks College in Rexburg, Idaho discussed whether or not members of the LDS church are required by God to be married.

"Honorable, happy, and successful marriage is surely the principal goal of every normal person. Marriage is designed of the Lord to make strong and happy homes and posterity. Anyone who would purposely avoid marriage is not only not normal, but is frustrating his own program.

I defend the term *normal* because the Lord set the norm Himself by bringing together Adam and Eve, his first male and first female on this earth, and performing a holy marriage ceremony to make them husband and wife. They were quite different in their makeup, with different roles to play. Hardly had he performed the ceremony then he said to them: "*Multiply, and replenish the earth, and subdue it: and have dominion*" (Gen. 1:28).

It is normal to marry and normal and proper to bear children. Every person should want and plan to be married because that is what God in Heaven planned for us. That is the way He worked it out.

If there is anyone who does not want to be married, who does not want a family, who says, "Oh, I am not going to

27 Bahr, Stephen J. "Mormon Statistics," *Light Planet*,
www.lightplanet.com/mormons/daily/social_eom.htm
(accessed 26 June 2014).

get married; I do not believe it is necessary," that is very, very shortsighted indeed.

It is disturbing to note how easily many people pass off this responsibility of marriage. Numerous people these days, as recorded in the magazines and newspapers, have sworn never to marry. They have found it much simpler and easier to live alone and have no responsibilities. That is why they will not ever grow big enough to become gods in eternity.

...No one who rejects the covenant of celestial marriage can reach exaltation in the eternal kingdom of God."[28]

Even at a young age, marriage is spoken of in high regard. In primary class, little Mormon boys and girls are taught to prepare themselves to be married in the temple for all eternity. I remember singing the song "Families Can Be Together Forever," proclaiming that I can spend eternity with my family through the power of a temple sealing.[29]

It is not difficult to see the pressure that is placed on every member of the LDS church to be married. They believe that God commanded it. Therefore, the LDS prophets enforce it, the churches stand by it, and the members live it. This is why most Mormons that you meet are either married or wanting to be. Within the LDS religion, whether or not a person should be married is not really up for discussion. The answer is a bold and deafening "Yes!"

---

[28] Kimball, Spencer W. "The Importance of Celestial Marriage" October 22, 1976
[29] Children's Songbook, "Families Can Be Together Forever." Gardner, Ruth Muir and Watkins, Vanja Y. 1980.

What Does the Bible
Say About Marriage

Do you really have to be married? Did God truly call every able bodied man and woman to marry? I would like to look to what the Bible has to say on the subject. The Bible says the apostle Paul was never married nor did he ever get married (1 Cor. 7:8). Paul even called his singleness a gift from God (1 Cor. 7:7). In fact, in his letter to the church in Corinth he said that single people have just as much of a place in ministry as do married couples. They both have a big role in God's plan. Either status can be useful. (1 Cor. 7:17-28). But according to LDS doctrine, only those who have entered into the holy covenant of marriage can see the Celestial Kingdom. If this were true, then the Apostle Paul would not be permitted entry into the highest kingdom of God.

Another biblical character that we should examine would be the prophet Jeremiah. God specifically told him never to marry and have children because they would *"die of deadly diseases"* (Jer. 16:1-2, 4). Yet Jeremiah is highly regarded as a prophet of God and is the author of several books in the Old Testament. However, if we are to believe Mormon scripture, Jeremiah is also exempt from entering into the highest degree of Heaven.

Who else is unmarried in the Bible? Miriam, Moses's sister, was never married. The prophet Elijah, who was so righteous that rather than die was taken up to Heaven in a chariot of fire (2 Kings 2:11), was never married. His predecessor Elisha, another prophet of Israel, was never married. John the Baptist, the prophet who spoke of Christ's coming (Matt. 3:11), was never married. There are several others that I have not even mentioned, but I will say one last name, the only one worth mentioning really, Jesus of Nazareth.

Jesus was never married. The first five books of the New Testament chronicle his life from five different perspectives. Not one mentions a wife, ever. One would think that this major piece of information regarding the Messiah's life would at least be mentioned once. When I have brought this up to several of my LDS friends in the past, they say, "Well just because the Bible never said it that does not mean He was never married." My argument to that would be to question then the importance of marriage. If not one of the gospels mentioned that Jesus may have been married, then is it even important? It seems contradictory that a topic seeming so vital to the LDS afterlife would not even be broached in the biography of Jesus' life. Furthermore, when Jesus was on the cross, He only asked for His mother to be taken care of (John 19:26-27). Would not a loving Husband request that His wife be provided for as well? All of this reaffirms that Jesus was never married. There is no account of such a major life event, nor was there any purpose for Jesus to be married.

When reading about His life, you realize that Jesus' main purpose for coming into this world was to save sinners (1 Tim. 1:15). His sole purpose on this earth was to die on the cross and redeem mankind for all eternity (Rom. 5:8-9). Jesus was purposeful in everything He did, always having God's will in mind. He would never do anything that would distract from His purpose nor delay Him in doing it. In fact, when Peter tried to reason with Jesus about dying on the cross, Jesus chastised him (Matt. 16:21-23). So if Peter was so quick to try and stop Jesus from dying on the cross, how much more so would a wife? Even if she was the most perfect example of a Proverbs 31 woman, I imagine *something* would have been said. This probably would have prompted Jesus to have the same reaction with His wife that He had with Peter. To me, this would be an unnecessary and constant burden.

Furthermore, Jesus was constantly on the move, traveling all over the Middle East, proselytizing and expanding the Kingdom of Heaven. How would He have found the time to provide for His wife? The Bible says it is a sin for a man to not provide for his family. *"But if any provide not for his own, and specially for those of his own house, he hath denied the faith, and is worse than an infidel"* (1 Tim. 5:8). But we know from scripture that Jesus was a traveler, and was constantly on the road preaching and performing miracles. This means that if He was married, then He was never around and therefore not able to provide for His family. However, Jesus is the ultimate provider thereby confirming even further that He was never married.

Lastly, the Jewish lineage was tracked meticulously. For example, we know that Jesus was a decedent of David, one through his mother Mary and the other as the adopted son of Joseph. We know the names of all the prophets and patriarchs in the Bible. While there is not an exhaustive list of women in the Bible, there is an account of some of the major players regarding the Jewish Nation. So then, it is logical to think that if Jesus did have a wife, it would be written down somewhere. It would not have been kept a secret. It is impossible to think that to this day, that would have been kept from us.

Why would Jesus get married? Being married would have done more to distract Him from His purpose than to help it. I believe then that we can claim with absolute certainty that Jesus Christ was never married.

So, that brings up the question, "Why do we marry?" If we do not have to get married then why do it? It is because marriage is a wonderful way to experience love, joy, companionship, intimacy, completeness, and teamwork. Furthermore, God uses marriage to refine us and turn us into better disciples of God. *"Iron sharpeneth iron; so a man sharpeneth the countenance of his friend"* (Prov. 27:17). Who better to know your weaknesses, see your shortcomings and your faults and lovingly help you overcome them than your spouse? They are the one person who spends life with you every day, who sees your struggles first hand, and are placed in the perfect position to make you a better person for Christ. This is why marriage is so great! It is an area that God can use to mold us into the person that He wants us to be (Prov. 17:3, Isa. 48:10). In addition, God uses marriage as a safe and healthy means to populate the earth. It is a way to express sexual desires while protecting us from sexual sin. Lust and immorality are always prevalent threats, but God in His infinite mercy has created the institution of marriage to safeguard us against such things.

With that being said, marriage is not for everyone. Some people simply have no desire to get married. God could have made them that way and they should in no way be ashamed of it. Some would acknowledge that He might have a different plan for their life and being single is the way to achieve it. Whatever the reason, the single life can be a righteous one. *"He that is unmarried careth for the things that belong to the Lord, how he may please the Lord...and this I speak...that ye may attend upon the Lord without distraction"* (1 Cor. 7:32b & 35b). To be unmarried allows you to be free from distractions and obligations and wholly serve the Lord, just as Jesus did. Furthermore, we as married Christ followers should encourage these men and women to fulfill God's will in their lives. We need to stop asking singles, "So, when do you think you will find Mr. or Mrs. Right?"

Let me sum up this way. Say you are moving across the country. You have to load up a moving van but have a choice to either drive by yourself or get someone to be your copilot/second driver. Clearly, neither one of these options is the wrong one. Some people like driving by themselves. They can listen to their own music as loud as they want without bothering anyone. They can make as many stops as they want and even meet up with friends for dinner on occasion. This person would reach their destination just fine and have a wonderful time getting there. On the other hand, there are some who just prefer to have someone else come along, preferably one that is cute and at least a decent driver. This way they would have someone to talk to on those boring stretches of road, someone to eat dinner with, and someone to help fix a flat tire. They too would arrive at their destination just fine and have a wonderful time getting there.

Marriage is that type of a relationship. My wife is my copilot. She helps steer me when I am off course from what God has commanded me. When I struggle, she is there to help support me and help shoulder my load. However, she does not determine whether I get into Heaven or not. She may help "steer" me on earth, but my final destination is based solely upon my relationship with Christ. We will greet each other in Heaven with a high five (because it will totally still be cool to do so) and say, "Glad to see you! Praise God we're here!" We will enjoy an eternity of praising our Lord and Savior, but only as individuals, not as a couple.

Where Is Jesus?

The belief in an eternal family is one that is commendable. It is a beautiful thought, truly. However, it overlooks the simple fact that we are here on this earth for the glory of God. Our spouse is not the main focus. Jesus is. With that being said, do not think that we will be placed in a supernatural isolation booth where only you and God exist. We will all be reunited in Heaven as a body of believers under His shelter of love and security. That is part of the joy of Heaven. We will see our family members again but not as family members, but rather as the body of Christ.

I had a discussion with my brother a while back regarding Heaven and eternal marriage. He told me that marriage is the greatest gift that our Heavenly Father could give us. Within the bond of an eternal marriage we can be confident that when we die our soul mate will be right next to us, sharing in the splendor of Heaven. He continued to say that when he dies he looks forward to the day that he will be reunited with his wife. His words were so sincere and heartfelt; I was honestly moved. He was not even married, yet he held the idea of his future wife in such high regard that it made me somewhat look at my own marriage and my relationship with my wife.

However, as I said before, Heaven is not about me or my wife. It is about Jesus. It is about giving honor and worship to Him who granted us eternal life. Though my brother's words were poetic, they lacked biblical authority. I in turn responded with a simple question, "What about Jesus?" I told him that I love my wife with all of my heart. I love her more than any other person on earth. She is my whole world. She makes every day just a little bit better simply by being in it. However, that love is infinitely overshadowed by my desire and joy to be face to face with my Lord and Savior.

Jesus says *"If any man come to me, and hate not his father, and mother, and wife, and children, and brethren, and sisters, yea, and his own life also, he cannot be my disciple"* (Luke 14:26). While it sounds harsh, Jesus is saying that our love for Him needs to be so great that the love in every other relationship might as well be hatred in comparison. We are commanded to give ourselves completely over to Him and elevate nothing and no one to His level.

In my experience, the majority of Mormons look forward to spending an eternity with their spouse, or their family, rather than spending it with Jesus. This is backwards. Jesus is the One who has given us eternal life and should, therefore, be first and foremost in our minds. By focusing on spending an eternity with their spouse instead of our God, Mormons have forgotten who truly deserves their honor and praise. While some Mormons may feel that looking forward to spending an eternity with their spouse is honoring their marriage, what they have actually done is turn their spouses, friends, or family members into an idol. These spouses have taken His place in their partner's hearts and have, therefore, been elevated above the Throne of Jesus.

What is even more disheartening is that there really is no reason for it. As I stated earlier, Heaven is a place where all believers will find rest. If our families are Christ followers we will see them again. The LDS church has broken God's holy command to accomplish what God has already set in place. I am so glad that God will allow me to see my wife, along with many other believers that have been taken home, when my time is up. However, please understand that Jesus is at the top of my list of people I am excited to see.

I told my brother that although my love for my wife is indescribable, my joy will come when I see my Savior face to face. I will cry and laugh all at the same time as I run into His arms and thank Him for saving me. All my life I only fell further into debt and yet He continued to offer me grace. For that I will fall at His feet in worship. This is something I look forward to immensely. What is even funnier is when I recounted this conversation with my wife a little later she laughed and told me the same thing. She asked, "Did you tell him that I feel the exact same way as you do? I mean, you are great and all, but you are not at all the first person I want to see when I get there."

The LDS Church places so much of an emphasis on marriage that they have completely overlooked who created it in the first place. Why would God create the LDS version marriage knowing that it completely removes Him from our desires and focus? Why would He make an institution that makes Him share His Glory with a sinful, created being? He would not.

Eternal marriage is contrary to what the Bible teaches. God is our Creator, and as such He requires that we give Him all the glory and honor. Throughout the Bible, God tells us to only worship Him, *"For the Lord thy God is a consuming fire, even a jealous God"* (Deut. 4:24). He commands us to not bow down or worship anything other than Him, for He alone is worthy of our praise (Exod. 20:5, Ps. 96:4).

Where is Jesus? The answer is, not where He should be. Jesus needs to be the focal point in our marriages. Without Him, it is just two sinful people trying not to fight. With Him there is purpose and direction. Jesus also needs to be the focal point in our singleness. *"And whatsoever ye do, do it heartily, as to the Lord, and not unto men"* (Col. 3:23). Jesus commands us to do everything to the joy of the Lord, which includes marriage and singleness. This means that no matter what is going on, you do your best in every relationship because He asked you to.

As long as every one of our relationships has Jesus at the head, we will be okay. Jesus is everything. Whether in our marriage or personal relationships He should always be the focus. My friends, I urge you to not set your eyes on anything else but Jesus. *"And the world passeth away, and the lust thereof: but he that doeth the will of God abideth for ever"* (I John 2:17).

Section Four:
Modern Day Prophets

"These are his words: 'I am going like a lamb to the slaughter; but I am calm as a summer's morning; I have a conscience void of offense towards God, and towards all men' (D&C 135:4). That statement of the Prophet teaches us obedience to law and the importance of having a clear conscience toward God and toward our fellowmen. The Prophet Joseph Smith taught these principles--by example.

'Greater love hath no man than this, that a man lay down his life for his friends' (John 15:13). The Prophet Joseph Smith taught us love--by example"

-Thomas S. Monson
16th President of the Church of Jesus Christ of Latter-day Saints
April 2014 General Conference

Leading the Way

One major characteristic of the LDS church that distinguishes it from other religions is the belief in modern day prophets. Most Bible believing churches are familiar with the idea of having a prophet because they recognize that there were prophets in the Old Testament. They do not believe though that there are any living prophets on the earth today. In contrast, Mormons believe that God has been continually providing prophets to guide their church since Joseph Smith. Their prophet, also called the president of the church, oversees any LDS doctrinal changes or revisions, manages where the church's resources go, and is ultimately responsible for the direction of the church as a whole. This role is a lifelong position. After a prophet passes away, the apostles and other leaders of the church privately pray and are given direction as to who the new prophet will be; very similar to how the Catholic Popes are chosen.

Biblically speaking, the idea of having and following a prophet is nothing new. Moses, for instance, is arguably one of the most famous prophets of the Old Testament. He was the mouthpiece of God, interceding on behalf of the Jewish Nation to be freed from Pharaoh's tyranny. He is just one of many prophets that are historically recognized as prophets of God. Today, these amazing men have been categorized as being either Major Prophets (those with a substantial amount of writing) or Minor Prophets (those with shorter writings). Either way, they were the men that God chose to communicate with in order to reveal His purpose to the world.

Now, there is a difference between being a prophet of God and having the gift of prophecy. God says in His word that anyone can be blessed with the gift of prophecy. *"But the manifestation of the Spirit is given to every man to profit withal. For to one is given by the Spirit...prophecy... But all these worketh that one and the selfsame Spirit, dividing to every man severally as he will"* (1 Cor. 12:7-11). This means that it is entirely possible for God to choose anyone to become His mouthpiece at any given time, even in the twenty-first century. This spiritual gift seems to manifests itself whenever God deems it necessary, on a sort of a case-by-case basis, so to speak. This though is not what is meant when Mormons discuss prophets.

Mormons instead believe the position of LDS prophet is a long-term role. The prophet is a man who was called by God and placed at the head of their church to provide continuous direction to His people. They are highly revered and given a great deal of influence. As such, God saw fit to warn us in several different places in His word about following false prophets. God tells us to examine their character (Matt 7:15-16) and determine if their worship is solely focused on God or not. For even if these proclaiming prophets are able to predict the future, perform miracles, or accomplish any other amazing feat, if they try to get us to take our focus off of God they are not to be trusted (Deut. 13:1-3).

This then will be our focus. We need to determine if these Mormon prophets are Christ-based. Under their leadership, guidance, and teaching, are they directing LDS members to worship and honor Jesus and no one else? Ultimately, is the church they are responsible for leading Christ-centered? These are the question we need to be able to answer.

Follow the Prophet,
Don't Go Astray

The LDS church teaches that they are "blessed to be led by living prophets-inspired men called to speak for the Lord...[and] the only person on the earth who receives revelation to guide the entire Church."[30] They speak directly to God and speak for God concerning His church. Sometimes God reveals a direction the church is to go. Other times God reveals to these men doctrinal nuances or changes that need to be made.

The LDS prophet is the ultimate authority here on earth. What these prophets say are widely considered by the LDS church to be doctrine. Twice a year, the prophet speaks to the entire worldwide church during an event called General Conference. Church based magazines often have articles quoting these talks as direct inspirations from God. Even parts of the Doctrine and Covenants, one of the LDS doctrinal books of scripture, are transcripts of speeches, spoken by previous modern day prophets. If a prophet speaks on the church's behalf, Mormons believe that it is God-breathed. LDS members are taught that they "...can always trust the living prophets. Their teachings reflect the will of the Lord...[and their] greatest safety lies in strictly following the word of the Lord given through His prophets, particularly the current President of the Church."[31]

I remember being told several times by church leaders and teachers that what the prophet says should be considered scripture. As such, I was taught that I could completely trust these men in their leadership for if they were to lead us astray God would have them removed immediately. God would not

---

[30] "Prophets," LDS, https://www.lds.org/topics/prophets
[31] *Same as footnote 13*

allow His church to be led away because of selfish intentions. That is why I have felt confident using excerpts and passages from the prophets' speeches when citing LDS doctrine. If the prophet says it, it is considered church doctrine.

The LDS prophets are also given absolute loyalty from their congregation. God commands all the LDS men and women to sustain and follow their prophet. This is actually a requirement before one can receive a Temple Recommend or the Priesthood. Their scriptures tell them that if they do not follow the prophet they, *"shall be cut off from among the people; for they have strayed from mine ordinances, and have broken mine everlasting covenant"* (D&C 1:14b-15). This though should not be alarming, for even in biblical times, the Lord wanted the people to follow His prophets. If God had something to say, He wanted His people to listen. Honestly, this devotion to their prophet is completely reasonable and commendable. If these men are indeed prophets of God, their words should absolutely be heard and heeded.

Coupled with their unwavering loyalty, LDS members also bestow upon these men a great deal of honor and reverence. I presume it is because they recognize the incredible weight that these me have to carry, as they are responsible for leading millions of members across the globe. As such, the LDS church does their best to lift them up and encourage them with adoration. This type of support can be seen even in today's society. We honor our fallen troops for their sacrifices for us, and for our country. We honor our loved ones when they pass away for how they impacted our lives. We honor Martin Luther King, Jr. for his work toward equal rights, as well as many other patriots for their dedication to equality.

This response even happened with the ancient prophets in the Old Testament. Many times in the Bible, characters are given honor and notoriety for their actions. The book of Numbers says that Moses was the most humble man on the face of the earth (Num. 12:3). The apostle Paul uses Abraham as an example of righteousness (Rom. 4:3, 9).

Out of all the prophets the LDS church has followed, none are revered and loved more than Joseph Smith. I say this because he is the only prophet the church refers to as 'beloved.' Joseph was the guy who got the proverbial ball rolling for the LDS church. It was his vision that eventually led to the creation of the Church of Jesus Christ of Latter-day Saints as well as the Book of Mormon. No other person is considered to have done more for the Church than Joseph Smith. It is because of this status that the next chapter is solely devoted to him and his legacy.

Joseph Smith

Obviously it would be virtually impossible to write a book about Mormonism and not discuss, at least in some regard, its founding father, Joseph Smith. However, I will not be talking about him in the way that you might think. I know that a lot of anti-Mormons will attack his prophecies and policies. These men and women would try to show whoever is willing to listen just where Mr. Smith was wrong. They would have documentation of certain things he said or wrote that is completely contrary to what they personally believe is correct. I will not do that in this book.

Some would look at who Joseph Smith was and attack his character. They would suppose that he was too young or too uneducated to write what the Book of Mormon purports to be. Some might even attack his marriage and his integrity by arguing the idea that he was a womanizer and a chauvinist. Some might go even further and look into who he was as a person, posing questions such as, 'was he well-liked?' or 'did he have many friends?' All of these topics I have read and researched, but they are not what I would like to focus on.

Again, the focus of this book is to try and answer the question, "Where is Jesus?" so that should be our compass. All of the above issues, again, are secondary. Once we answer the main question all other inquiries should fall into place.

So, what I would like to do is look at Joseph Smith's legacy. How do Mormons perceive Joseph Smith today? What do the members have to say about the "beloved" prophet? It is when we answer these questions that the answer to our primary question will be revealed.

Let us look into a song that can be found in the LDS hymnal. Thomas S. Monson, the current president of the LDS church, says that during his first meeting with the leaders of the church they sang a hymn entitled, "Praise to the Man", a song that honors the first modern day prophet. Monson stated, "[The] hymn which we sang, honoring Joseph Smith, the Prophet, was and is a favorite of mine."[32]　Below are the lyrics to that very song.

Praise to the Man
By: William W. Phelps

Praise to the man who communed with Jehovah!
Jesus anointed that Prophet and Seer.
Blessed to open the last dispensation,
Kings shall extol him, and nations revere.

Praise to his mem'ry, he died as a martyr;
Honored and blest be his ever great name!
Long shall his blood, which was shed by assassins,
Plead unto heav'n while the earth lauds his fame.

Great is his glory and endless his priesthood.
Ever and ever the keys he will hold.
Faithful and true, he will enter his kingdom.
Crowned in the midst of the prophets of old.

Sacrifice brings forth the blessings of heaven;
Earth must atone for the blood of that man.
Wake up the world for the conflict of justice.
Millions shall know "Brother Joseph" again.

Hail to the Prophet, ascended to heaven!
Traitors and tyrants now fight him in vain
Mingling with Gods, he can plan for his brethren;
Death cannot conquer the hero again.

---

[32] Monson, Thomas S. "The Prophet Joseph Smith: Teacher by Example," General Conference, April 2014.

"Praise to the man" is a bold title. Joseph is a man, which we know are all sinners in need of a savior. Yet, the song lifts him higher and higher as it progresses. The hymnist says that "Kings shall praise him, nations revere" him. Congregations sing "Honored and blest be [Joseph's] ever great name!" with a loud cry. They all praise Joseph Smith by saying in the third verse that his glory is great and his authority is endless and it is because of his righteousness that he will enter his kingdom, seated rightfully amidst the crowd of biblical prophets.

The last and final verse I believe is where it goes above and beyond. "Earth must atone for the blood of that man." These words convey an idea that He was chosen and precious, thus making his blood sacred. Are you beginning to see a parallel?

Do not get me wrong though. Any time there is a life that is taken, it is sad and wrong. The fact that Joseph Smith was assassinated in his jail cell in Carthage, Illinois is a tragedy. No matter what anyone says, that was a vicious crime and should never have happened. Regardless of how you feel about him, he was a man whom Jesus cared about and chose to die for. With that being said, it is concerning that the LDS church believes the earth must atone for his blood. He was a sinner just like you and me. In God's eyes, he was no better than any of us, or than any of his assassins were.

The very last line is what all the previous verses lead up to; it is the crescendo of the lyrics. "Millions shall know 'Brother Joseph' again". Now, I do not know if these "millions" refer to the multi-millions of members within the LDS church or to the elect that will be allowed admittance into the celestial kingdom. Either way, this song does not focus on the person it should. This hymn, and frankly every hymn, should be about Jesus. This one is not. It does not praise Jesus, nor does it even mention Jesus. Instead it praises and elevates a mere man, Joseph Smith. Should not Jesus be the crescendo? Should not millions know who Jesus is?

Some Mormons might say, "Well that's only one song! We have hundreds of songs that praise God. It's not even a close race! Jesus is obviously the main focus. We simply honor our prophet for what he did!" To them I would ask that they truly look at the lyrics and see it for what it really is. It is very obvious that these words go far beyond that of just remembering and honoring Joseph. Instead, these words drift dangerously along the lines of praise and worship. Furthermore, even if this is the only song that worships Joseph Smith, that is still one song too many. The Bible says that God should be the lone receiver of our worship, for He is a jealous God (Exod. 20:5, 34:14, Deut. 4:24, Josh. 24:19). Remember His response to the Israelites when they worshipped the golden calf? (Exod. 32:19-29). Remember His response to His chosen people when they forsook Him and instead worshipped Baal? (Judges 2:10-15). He should absolutely be the only one we sing praises to. Period.

Worse still is that this song is not just about praising Joseph, but it draws parallels between Jesus and Joseph. These parallels are undeniable and create a sense of equality between the two of them. Now let me be painfully clear here, no one is even remotely on the same playing field as Jesus Christ. That is why Jesus is so deserving of our praise. If anyone could do what He did for the entire world then He would cease to be praise worthy. The Bible says that the level of praise the Mormons are giving to Joseph Smith should only be bestowed upon Jesus.

2 Samuel 22:50
Therefore I will give thanks unto thee, O Lord, among the heathen, and I will sing praises unto thy name

Psalm 150:3-6
Praise him with the sound of the trumpet, praise him with the psaltery and harp. Praise him with the timbrel and dance: praise him with stringed instruments and organs. Praise him upon the loud cymbals: praise him

upon the high sounding cymbals. Let every thing that hath breath praise the Lord. Praise ye the Lord.

Remember when I said that the prophets of old were honored and revered by the people? What should also be noted is that the prophets always directed their worship and praise upward. In Exodus, Moses led the Israelites in a song to the Lord (Exod. 15:1). King David told everyone to give praises to the Lord (1 Chron. 16:8). The fact that the succeeding LDS prophets of God allow anyone else to receive praise other than God is, for lack of a better word, astounding. It is not difficult to see that God is not the only object of praise within the Mormon Church.

Proverbs 27:21 says that praise reveals the true heart of a person. If they are humble and subservient to God, they will graciously and lovingly direct all praise upward. I have a friend who is one of these types of people. Every time I commend him for his worship and thank him for the blessing that he is in my life his reaction is always the same. He smiles, almost like a kid opening a Christmas present, and he says, "Praise God! Amen!" His words and actions communicate to me and everyone else that God used him for His purpose and he was just so grateful to be used. We should all follow my friend's example. When we receive honors and accolades we must graciously redirect them to Him.

Lastly, I would like to direct you to a relevant passage of LDS scripture:

D&C 135:3
Joseph Smith, the Prophet and Seer of the Lord, has done more, save Jesus only, for the salvation of men in this world, than any other man that ever lived in it. In the short space of twenty years, he has brought forth the Book of Mormon, which he translated by the gift and power of God, and has been the means of publishing it on two continents; has sent the fullness of the everlasting

gospel, which it contained, to the four quarters of the earth; has brought forth the revelations and commandments which compose this book of Doctrine and Covenants, and many other wise documents and instructions for the benefit of the children of men; gathered many thousands of the Latter-day Saints, founded a great city, and left a fame and name that cannot be slain. He lived great, and he died great in the eyes of God and his people; and like most of the Lord's anointed in ancient times, has sealed his mission and his works with his own blood.."

I cannot help but draw parallels between this scripture and what John Lennon said in 1966. John Lennon stated that because of the decline in Christianity in the world the Beatles had become "more popular than Jesus."[33] This is precisely the mentality I am urging everyone to stay away from. Nothing and no one is equal with Jesus, including Joseph Smith. Jesus is greater than everyone and everything because in Him were all things created (Col. 1:16). No one even comes close to the glory of God. And if we as His creations lift up idols, whether they are golden calves or prophets of a church, it is a sin and we need to repent of it.

33 "More popular than Jesus," Wikipedia. Accessed April 4, 2014.
    http://en.widipedia.org/wiki/More_popular_than_Jesus

Where is Jesus?

God's prophets were completely loyal to Him. These men ensured that He received all the glory. My point throughout this entire section is that Mormon prophets, either by their own doing or by allowing the church to do it, are elevated to or above the throne of Jesus. The LDS prophets have therefore stepped in and received for themselves some of His glory and honor. This, in turn, dishonors the One who deserves it most. If these men were true prophets of God, the LDS church's focus would never be on any of them. Instead, it would be on Jesus one-hundred percent of the time (Deut. 13:1-3). Unfortunately, this is just not the case. We have seen that LDS prophets, namely Joseph Smith, are often the targets of praise and worship.

Tom Mercer, Senior Pastor of High Desert Church, says, "We need to keep the main thing the main thing." It is not that these men should not be admired and revered as leaders. That, in and of itself, is not a sin. We should honor our leaders, presidents, parents, teachers, and employers because of the significant roles that they play in our lives. The problem only arises when that admiration turns into praise and ultimately places the recipient on equal ground with Jesus. Again, this should never happen, in any church. No one is equal to Him, nor will anyone ever be. That is why He alone is deserving of our hearts and minds.

Whether or not you are Mormon, the idea of constructing idols and worshipping them is an issue that we all need to be wary of. In the case of the LDS church, they have taken a beautiful gift from God, such as the leadership of a prophet, and placed them on pedestals. What is even more damaging is that these prophets seem to allow it and, at times, propagate it even further. Not once have I ever heard anyone in the Church say that the song "Praise to the Man" should not be sung. Nor do I hear these LDS prophets reminding their people that "... *The servant is not greater than his lord; neither he that is sent greater than he that sent*" (John 13:16). Instead, these men are regarded as celebrities and elevated as such, with Joseph Smith in the top tier. Members of the church do not seem to be bothered by this fact, or even willing to admit it. "Praise to the Man" and any other song that does not bestow all glory, honor, and power to Jesus Christ should be ripped out of the hymnal for its heresy.

Sadly, the phenomenon of elevating people of stature and ability to a sinful level is not uncommon in our culture. I have even seen hints of it in my own church. Pastors and worship leaders are sometimes held in reverence above the "common" believer because they hold positions of status. They are using their God-given talents every week and in front of the entire congregation. This tends to prompt people in the church to elevate and treat them differently. This reverence manifests itself when we see them in public or off stage and we get butterflies and giddy around them. We sometimes view these men and women as Christian 'celebrities' which makes them seem somehow better or greater than the rest of the church family. This is a mistake bordering on idolatry.

What we as the body of Christ need to realize is that these gifts are no more important to the body of Christ than those blessed with hospitality, prayer, or any other dozens of endowments (1 Cor. 12:4-6). It is essential then that no matter what role you play in the Body, we all should point to the head, who is Christ. The apostle Paul says "*For as the body is one, and hath many members, and all the members of that one body, being many, are one body: so also is Christ....For the body is not one member, but many*" (1 Cor. 12:12, 14).

King David wrote, "*Search me, God, and know my heart; try me...see if there be any wicked way in me, and lead me in the way everlasting*" (Psalm 139:23-24). I challenge the reader to follow King David's lead and honestly pray this prayer for themselves. Ask God to reveal who in your life is taking Jesus' rightful place. Ask Him to search your heart to help you determine if your praises are misguided. Ask if you have broken His commandments by creating an idol above the One who is most worthy of your praise (Psalm 145:3). The great thing is that God is merciful and He is quick to forgive. The Bible says that "*if we confess our sins, he is faithful and just to forgive us our sins, and to cleanse us from all unrighteousness*" (1 John 1:9).

Section Five:
The Holy Scriptures

"In the council with the Twelve Apostles, Joseph Smith said, 'I told the brethren that the Book of Mormon was the most correct of any book on earth, and the keystone of our religion, and a man would get nearer to God by abiding by its precepts, than by any other book.'"

-Franklin D. Richards
Apostle of the Church of Jesus Christ of Latter-day Saints
A Compendium of the Doctrines of the Gospel - *p. 273*

One Plus Three

The Bible is a book that all professed Christians hold very dear to their heart. Within its pages lie the answers to life's toughest questions. Where did I come from? Where am I going? Why am I here? What happens after you die? All of these and many others can be answered simply by reading God's word.

Mormons also believe that the Bible is the word of God. The only difference is that they do not believe that it is the only book in which God has spoken. In fact, they believe that those who rely solely on the Bible are missing the bigger picture.

> 2 Nephi 29:6-10
>
> *"Thou fool, that shall say: A Bible, we have got a Bible, and we need no more Bible. Have ye obtained a Bible save it were by the Jews? Know ye not that there are more nations than one? ... I bring forth my word unto the children of men, yea, even upon all the nations of the earth? Wherefore murmur ye, because that ye shall receive more of my word? Know ye not that the testimony of two nations is a witness unto you that I am God, that I remember one nation like unto another?...And because that I have spoken one word ye need not suppose that I cannot speak another; for my work is not yet finished; neither shall it be until the end of man, neither from that time and henceforth and forever. Wherefore, because that ye have a Bible ye need not suppose that it contains all my words; neither need ye suppose that I have not cause more to be written."*

This then is the Mormon perspective on scripture: God has indeed spoken in the Bible but He has not been silent since its completion. It is out of His great love for us that He has remained in contact with His creation and is continually giving information and guidance.

It is because of this belief that the LDS church recognizes three other books as being revelations of God. They state these other scriptures are just as much the Word of God as is the Bible, and therefore speak with just as much authority. Currently, the LDS church has uses the King James Version of the Bible, the Doctrine and Covenants, the Pearl of Great Price, and the Book of Mormon. These four books make up what is commonly called the standard works of the LDS church.

The Standard Works

The opening pages of Doctrine and Covenants, or D&C as it is commonly called, say that it "is a collection of divine revelations and inspired declarations given for the establishment and regulation of the kingdom of God on the earth in the last days. ...Most of the revelations in this compilation were received through Joseph Smith Jr...Others were issued through some of his successors in the Presidency" (D&C Introduction). These are not translations of old manuscripts or writings, but rather modern day revelations from the time of Joseph Smith and forward. Since the LDS church believes these writings are penned interactions with God they have no doubt as to their validity or authority.

The Pearl of Great Price contains revelations given to the prophet Joseph Smith regarding some writings of the Bible as well as more direction to the LDS church. Within its pages contain Joseph Smith's translation of the book of Genesis, translations of ancient Egyptian papyri presumed to be the writings of Abraham, translations of parts of the Apostle Matthew's gospel, an autobiography of Joseph Smith, and the LDS's creed which is often referred to as the Articles of Faith.

The last LDS scripture, probably the most famous out of all the others, is the Book of Mormon. It is believed to have been written on golden plates of brass. The LDS members claim that it contains the records of two groups of people. The first group, the Jaredites, came straight from the time of Babel, when God confused the languages and scattered the people all across the earth. This account can be found in Genesis 11:8. The second group came from Jerusalem at around 600 BC. This group eventually split into two nations and are referred to as the Nephites and the Lamanites. The Book of Mormon also claims to have another account of the ministry of Jesus Christ, after His resurrection.

All of these writings were composed by men, most of who were considered to be prophets. Eventually, all of these writing were compiled by the Nephite prophet Mormon. This is how the book acquired its name. Before Mormon died, he handed this book down to his son Moroni, who hid it in the Hill Cumorah to prevent this record from being destroyed. On September 21, 1823 Moroni appeared to Joseph Smith and revealed the location of this record. Joseph then translated each word by the power of God and gave the world the first edition of the Book of Mormon. "The Book of Mormon is a volume of holy scripture comparable to the Bible. It is a record of God's dealings with ancient inhabitants of the Americas and contains the fullness of the everlasting gospel" (Book of Mormon, Introduction).

Now, many anti-Mormons would sit back and debate whether these books were actual historical accounts or not. But the point of this book is not to debate Mormon doctrine nor question the validity of their scripture. Again, the focus of this book is to try and find Jesus. But, we have already seen that the Mormon Jesus, the one spoken of in the LDS scriptures, is vastly different from the Biblical Jesus. So what else is there to talk about?

To prevent these next few chapters from being another recap I will instead speak on the point of Biblical authority. Since God is never changing (Mal. 3:6, Heb. 13:8) then He is also always relevant. This means that the Bible will never, in a matter of speaking, go out of style. It also means that regardless of future revelations, the Bible is and always should be trustworthy. Furthermore, any other book from God should be in perfect harmony with the original book.

Accordingly, all three of the LDS books are said to in fact work hand in hand with the Bible. For instance, the Book of Mormon says of itself on the cover that it is another testament of Jesus Christ. It does not claim to replace the Bible but work in tangent with it. All Mormons will claim without fail that the Bible is just as important as these other books.

If the LDS church has indeed found additional writings that are God-breathed then should not these new findings be just as valued as the Bible? It makes sense to think that a loving God would not have created the Bible, His first revelation, to somehow become obsolete. An all knowing God would not have created a book that needed to be re-written, revised, or eventually discarded. As such, His first book would be as true today as it was 2000 years ago. This is what the Mormons claim to believe. However, their claim and their doctrine and practices tell two different stories.

The Eighth Article

I need the reader to understand that the Articles of Faith are considered to be the LDS's creed, or their statements of faith. They are not to be taken lightly or thought of as just general ideas for the church. They are thirteen statements that absolutely outline a Mormon's faith and represent core beliefs. They were something that as a kid I was constantly encouraged to memorize by my superiors. My teachers and Sunday school leaders would lead my primary class in songs and have us do different activities to try and help us commit these thirteen statements to memory. Let us look now look at the one article of faith which touches upon the subject of Biblical authority.

The eighth article of faith states, *"We believe the Bible to be the word of God as far as it is translated correctly; we also believe the Book of Mormon to be the word of God"* (Articles of Faith 1:8). At first glance, this statement does not strike any chords in the casual reader. Even as a Mormon, I saw nothing wrong with this statement at all as it was just a declaration that the Bible and the Book of Mormon are both the word of God. However, once removed from the LDS church I began to notice an inconsistency with what I thought this statement said and what the Mormon Church taught. Time and time again I noticed that Mormons rely heavily on the Book of Mormon and very little on the Bible when either discussing or defending their faith. This seemed odd to me since the LDS claim to use them both in tandem. If Mormons believe them both to be the word of God then why not use them equally?

Eventually, I began to notice more and more the phrase *"as far as it is translated correctly."* It never really bothered me growing up because the King James translation (which is the only version the LDS church supports) is sometimes very difficult to understand. Even as an adult I struggle with that particular translation sometimes just because the language used is partly foreign. Whenever I read the KJV and it did not make sense with some portion of LDS doctrine I thought the problem was with me. Maybe I was translating it incorrectly. I know that I am not the only one who thought this way. In fact, I am willing to bet there are some who are reading this right now who have felt the same way.

It is true that we need to read the Bible very carefully, humbly, and prayerfully, whilst being mindful to context, culture, and language. However, after I left the church and really started to research everything, I realized something very troubling. By stating *"as far as it is translated correctly,"* Mormons are given the liberty to reinterpret the Bible to fit what the Book of Mormon teaches. This mistaken hierarchy is taught to Mormons at an early age and cultivated as the years go on. As a result, when deep theological conversations occur with non-Mormons and biblical truth is presented, LDS members can respond by simply stating that the accuser has the wrong interpretation of Holy Scripture.

I have had this exact thing happen to me many, many times. I would be talking to a Mormon friend or family member about the nature of Jesus, or about Heaven, or even salvation (most of which I have written about in this book) and I would use quotes from the Bible to back up my argument. They would in turn simply respond by saying that my interpretation of scripture is wrong. Accepting the fact that I am not a Bible scholar, I would invite them to explain to me where I am wrong. I would ask that they show me how the passage I am using is either being taken out of context or that it could reasonably mean anything other than what I was saying. My hope was that they would sit with me and start a healthy conversation to try and understand Biblical truth.

Their responses would vary. Some of my friends would try and explain to me how the Bible has changed so many times over the years and thus it can no longer be used as an absolute authority. In fact, this is exactly what the LDS scriptures teach its members. *"Wherefore, thou seest that after the book hath gone forth through the hands of the great and abominable church, that there are many plain and precious things taken away from the book, which is the book of the Lamb of God...[and] because of these things which are taken away out of the gospel of the Lamb, an exceedingly great many do stumble, yeah, insomuch that Satan hath great power over them."* (1 Nephi 13:28-29). Mormons are taught that the Bible has lost its integrity over the years and therefore cannot be fully trusted. They believe that because of an apostasy within God's church the authority from His written word has been removed.

Other responses were simply to push me away and proclaim that they have a living prophet who agrees with their argument and not mine. They would tell me that they just know that what they believe is true and that I just simply do not understand. One person in particular added that I was too delusional to talk to, and he deemed me, "hopeless." These types of responses can be the most frustrating. I have found that they leave little to no room for truth to function. Walls are immediately put up and the discussion has basically ended.

So you see, it does not matter for most Mormons if the Bible is very clear or concise. If it seems to conflict with LDS doctrine, then the only explanation is that the Bible is either not being interpreted correctly or since it has corrupted over the years it is no longer the authority on the matter. The belief of Biblical inaccuracy has become a full proof scapegoat that often needs God's intervention to overcome.

Did you notice though that the Book of Mormon has no such clause? This article of faith casually states that the Book of Mormon is simply regarded as *"the word of God."* There is no need to worry about proper interpretation or translation. It is not even questionable in the least. By not giving the Book of Mormon any type of clarifier (i.e. – *"as far as it is translated correctly)*, Mormons have essentially stated that the Book of Mormon is completely correct and trustworthy while the Bible is not. This little nuance elevates the authority of the Book of Mormon to that above the Bible.

The Bible,
Version 2.0

In the previous chapter, we discussed that Mormons perceive the Bible as being incomplete. So, logic would dictate that in order to 'fix' the Bible what was changed and/or removed would need to be corrected. Mormons believe that God has done precisely this through the prophet Joseph Smith. "The Lord inspired the Prophet Joseph to restore truths to the Bible text that had been lost or changed since the original works were written. These inspired corrections are called the Joseph Smith Translation of the Bible."[34] In the Joseph Smith Translation (JST) of the Bible the books Genesis, Exodus, 1st Chronicles, Psalms, Isaiah, Matthew, Mark, Luke, John, the Book of Acts, Romans, 1st Corinthians, Galatians, Colossians, 2nd Thessalonians, First Timothy, Hebrews, James, 2nd Peter, and Revelations have all been 'corrected.' This translation, although offering "many interesting insights and (being) an invaluable aid to biblical interpretation and understanding," it is not the official Bible the LDS church uses from day to day. It does however, remain as a crucial asset to the church in helping to restore the truths and wisdom that have been lost in today's Bible.[35]

What many LDS members do not understand is that the Bible has been tested against ancient manuscripts and the Dead Sea scrolls in order to validate its reliability. What is so amazing is that scholars actually found that the integrity of the Bible is indeed still intact! These scholars have given us enough confidence to be able to say firmly that the Bible today contains the same amount of truth and authority that it did when it was

---

[34] *Gospel Principles* (The Church of Jesus Christ of Latter-day Saints, 2011), 44-49.
[35] *Bible Dictionary: Joseph Smith Translation (JST)* (The Church of Jesus Christ of Latter-day Saints).

written. Praise God! Unfortunately, this finding seemingly contradicts with Joseph Smith's supposed calling from God to re-translate it. So, since the Bible is in fact trustworthy, why would God have the need for someone to rewrite so many of its books?

I can remember when I was a young Mormon being presented with the scripture "*Ye shall not add unto the word which I command you, neither shall ye diminish ought from it, that ye may keep the commandments of the Lord your God which I command you*" (Deut. 4:2). To which I would respond with two arguments. The first argument is that when Deuteronomy, or Proverbs, or even the New Testament was written, the Bible, meaning the entire book from Genesis to Revelation, did not even exist. As such the writers could not have possibly been referring to the Bible as a whole. Any warnings regarding changes or additions were simply meant for those individual books or writings. The second argument I would give was that Mormonism does not add, or change, the meaning of the Bible. I would say, "Our faith and our scriptures enhance what the Bible teaches."

However, from where I stand now these two arguments do not hold water. While it is true that the Bible was not combined at the time it was penned, God knew it was one day going to be. Thus, in His infinite wisdom, He had the writers place into His Word the command to not add or change anything. Furthermore, the writers of the Bible were actually trying to prevent anyone from changing the substance of what they felt God was prompting them to write by adding these warnings. The LDS church, through the JST, has taken the Bible and rewritten it to say what they want their members to believe. They have hypocritically done what they mistakenly condemn the rest of the world for doing. (Remember their argument against me in the last chapter?) They have taken out what they felt did not fit with their belief systems and inserted what did. This can be easily seen in their doctrine concerning Jesus and the afterlife (section 1 and section 2 of this book, respectively).

Along with the notion that the Bible is infallible, Mormons are encouraged not to listen to, read, or participate in any form of anti-Mormon propaganda. So while they can absolutely question the Bible, they leave no room to question their own scriptures or doctrine. They think that since they have the truth they do not need to confuse themselves with any outside doctrine as it would only invite opportunities for Satan to deceive and lead them away from the true Church. To which I can only reply with Holy Scripture:

> 1 Thess. 5:19-22
> *Quench not the Spirit. Despise not prophesyings. Prove all things; hold fast that which is good. Abstain from all appearance of evil.*

God tells us to test everything, including what He has told us. Test it with prayer, with our minds, and among our circle of believers to ensure that what is being told to us is from Him. He tells us this so we can escape from closed mindedness and from being stagnant in our faith. Instead, he gives us the opportunity to grow, improve, and further our understanding of Him. How can we do this if we only read what is given to us in Church? How can we preach to a world of non-believers if we do not know what those non-believers believe? I myself have read, watched, and listened to a vast amount of non-Christian literature. I did this not because my faith was shaky, but because I want to be prepared to give an account of why I believe the way that I do (1 Peter 3:15).

Where Is Jesus?

The Bible is often referred to as the word of God. What you may not realize is that Jesus is also referred to as the Word. *"In the beginning was the Word, and the Word was with God, and the Word was God"* (John 1:1). So even though we have been looking at the written word in these last few chapters, in truth we have been looking at Jesus all along. The Bible contains His written word, and speaks with just as much authority as if Jesus was speaking them Himself. As such, as long as the authority of the Bible is upheld, the message of the Bible is not altered, and Jesus Christ is Lord of all, then Jesus is where He should be.

Christians believe the Bible to be the word of God. Since God is the supreme, omnipotent Creator, anything He has revealed should always be considered as the supreme authority. Even if God was to reveal other books or revelations, the first revelation is still just as important because it comes from God. Take any computer program for example. The first version is good, but then a few bugs are found and updates are needed. Programmers then rewrite the code to account for these oversights and produce a new version called 2.0. Again, as time goes on, more and more bugs are found, prompting newer and better versions to be made. Thankfully, God is not like this at all. Everything He makes is the best possible version and has no defects in it whatsoever. His versions are perfect the first time, every time. This is how we should view the Bible.

Mormons though do not see the Bible as having this quality. While they do incorporate its teachings in their doctrine, they interpret the Bible to say what they need it to say in order to justify their beliefs because they believe it is corrupt. The LDS church has in turn created a religion in which the only books that you can truly rely on are their own. Sadly, within the LDS scriptures you find a doctrine that is not only vastly different than that of the Biblical gospel of Jesus Christ but also ideas that border on heresy. Yet, since members are not allowed to question their church's doctrines or views they, in turn, drift further and further away from Jesus. This drifting has gone on for so long that today, Mormons not only have a distorted view of the gospel of salvation but also perceive the Bible not as God's Holy Word but rather a really good book.

What we need to always remember is that Jesus wrote the Bible. Even though many human writers penned it, God is the author. Furthermore, He makes it very clear, in His Word, that He cannot lie (Num. 23:19). Deceit is not in His character, thus making it impossible for Him to mislead us. Therefore, if another book claimed to be written by Him it would need to work in perfect accord with His already existing Word. However, throughout this book we have seen that there are major theological differences between Mormonism and Christianity. This means then that the Bible, where Christianity receives its doctrine, and the Book of Mormon and other LDS scriptures, where Mormons get their theology, do not work "hand in hand." As such, the LDS scriptures cannot be considered to be God breathed. Simply put, God is not the author of the Mormon scriptures and they should not be considered Holy.

In effect, the LDS church has placed one more thing above the throne of God, and that is their scriptures. Their beloved Book of Mormon, Doctrine and Covenants, Pearl of Great Price, and the JST Bible have replaced His holy word as the ultimate authority, thereby removing Jesus from the head of the church. His Word and, more importantly, His self are no longer what they look to for answers. God then has been stripped of His headship as King of Kings in the LDS church.

I urge you my friends, do not raise this idol before your God. Let the Bible, which is His righteous word, be the ultimate authority in your life. No matter what you do, no matter which religious books you read, always compare and test it against the Bible.

Lastly, the Bible has been validated scientifically and linguistically by several experts. We therefore have full confidence that what is being read today is true to what was written thousands of years ago. As of yet, there have not been any scientific breakthroughs that would validate the Book of Mormon. If anyone is still on the fence regarding whether or not to trust either the Book of Mormon or the Bible, I urge you to do some of your own research and find the answers for yourself. Research both sides of this argument. Do not just take my word for it, or your pastor's word or your bishop's word or anyone else's. Find out for yourself. Use your God-given mind and really do some objective research. We live in an age where information is at your fingertips. Why not use this technology to help you grow closer to God and worship Him fully? The wonderful thing about our God is He loves to reveal Himself to anyone who is searching. Do not let your own bias cloud your judgment. Be in constant prayer, asking God for guidance and instruction on everything you come across. You will be glad you did.

Section Six: Conclusion

"My plea is that as we continue our search for truth, particularly we of the Church, that we look for strength and goodness rather than weakness and foibles in those who did so great a work in their time. ...I do not fear truth. I welcome it. But I wish all of my facts to be in their proper context"

-Gordon B. Hinkley
15th President of the Church of Jesus Christ of Latter-day Saints
"The Continuing Pursuit of Truth," Ensign, April 1986, p.4-6

Hear "I AM"

In my research, I have found that the foundational beliefs in which the LDS church is built upon do not glorify Jesus. While Jesus is a focal point, He is not *the* focal point. There are at least four major topics that I have outlined in this book that have been placed either above or on equal playing ground as our Lord and Savior, Jesus Christ. The aspiration for exaltation, their marriages, their prophets, and their standard works of scripture all share the throne with, or dethrone entirely, Jesus. But perhaps the most important problem that I have found is that the actual Jesus to whom they worship is not the Biblical one.

Though Mormons have incorporated His name into their title, they have missed who He is completely. Jesus should be the center of every piece of doctrine that comes out. Every word spoken from the pulpit should be drenched in His grace, truth, and mercy. However, as we have continually seen throughout this book this is not the case. If Jesus was truly at the center of the LDS church, then all of their doctrines, practices, beliefs, and creeds would show that (Matt. 7:20). We would be able to see Jesus everywhere and anywhere we looked in the LDS church, but the truth is, we do not.

Any religion that does not have Christ at its center sooner or later will fail. Though the LDS church is a multi-billion dollar organization with close to sixteen million members worldwide, Christ is not at the helm. It does not matter how many members you have if Jesus is not one of them. In the case of the Mormon Church, Jesus has taken a backseat to virtually every core belief the LDS church has and as a result, it will eternally fail.

The whole point of this book is to get people to recognize whether or not they have placed our Savior at the center of their worship by asking one simple question, "Where is Jesus?" All other fathomable religious issues are absolutely secondary to the placement of Jesus in your life. Jesus is the most important person that you can ever encounter in your lifetime. No other person on the face of the earth even comes close. The Bible says there is no other name given that can save you except Jesus (Acts 4:12).

Jesus wants to have a relationship with you. That should be priority number one. Where you park your car or whether you wear a suit or flip-flops on Sunday morning, in the grand scheme of life, is not important. Only your relationship with the living God is. It will transform you so that when those secondary and tertiary issues come up you have a focal point with which to guide you. Luckily this relationship is not up to any church to decide. Regardless of what religion you are, it is your choice whether or not you wish to have a relationship with Him. It is entirely possible to consider yourself a Mormon and have Jesus at the center of your life. I cannot stress this enough. No matter what "religion" you claim, as long as Jesus is your Lord and Savior you will be saved for all eternity. This is because the gospel has always been about a relationship, not a membership. However, be warned. You can also attend a church that doctrinally has Jesus at the head and still lose your soul for all eternity. Again, if you do not know Jesus personally, then you will spend an eternity in Hell.

Just ask yourself, "Does Jesus form who I am as a person? Has he formed the chambers of my heart?" At the end of the day, when it is all said and done, these questions are all that matter. You need to determine whether or not Jesus is where He should be in your life.

To My LDS Brothers and Sisters

If you are Mormon, I would urge you to take a long, hard look at your relationship with Jesus. Examine your core beliefs and see if Jesus is at the center. What is your main goal in life here on earth? Who is your main focus? This is not up to me or anyone else to decide. This question is between you and our Savior.

Do not be concerned with whether or not you will become a god when you get to Heaven. Instead, recognize that when we die it will be a blessing to just be in His presence. Understand that our sin has separated us from God and set us on a crash course to that place of fiery torment. It is only through the blood of Jesus Christ that we can escape this fate and live with Him in Heaven. Heaven is a gift and a privilege, not an entitlement. The belief that you or anyone else has even the potential to become a god means that you believe to live with God eternally is not a good enough reward. Instead you want His throne, His glory, and His power. This is something that Satan craved and what led to his banishment. Do not be guilty of the same sin. God is God and He alone sits enthroned (Isa. 37:16).

If and when you are married, your marriage should be intently focused on Jesus. Who do you want to be with when you get to Heaven? Though you may want to see your significant other in Heaven, which the Bible says you can (though not as a married couple), the desire to rest safely in your Savior's arms should be your biggest desire. Furthermore, ensure that your marriage is a beacon to your kids, friends, and family that points directly to the Jesus. If, instead, you decide to go the single route then be joyful in the Lord in that decision as well. Being single does not mean the focus is different, just the way you express it is. Get involved in ministry, go serve on long term missions to foreign countries, or do whatever God places on your heart to further His Kingdom.

We can all agree that the LDS prophets, apostles, and leaders of the church are loving, kind, and genuine people that should be treated with respect. I truly believe that they are not trying to lead anyone astray. But even if everything they say was one-hundred percent accurate, the fact they allow themselves to be viewed even remotely equal to Jesus is wrong. Biblical prophets always pointed to Jesus. In the book of Genesis, when Joseph was asked to interpret Pharaoh's dream he replied, "*Do not interpretations belong to God?*" (Gen 40:8b). Joseph did not take one ounce of credit for his gift but instead gave God all the glory. It is because of his faithfulness that he was blessed. Angels time and time again always give praise to God. As such, the leaders of any church should also be this humble. They should never be worshiped nor allow anyone to worship them, even in the slightest. That position of honor only has room for one.

The Bible is the true and living word of God. It overshadows any other book that has ever been made. Ask yourself if you believe that the Bible is truly the word of God? Do you see it as a book that needs clarification or revision? I find it kind of funny how some people can believe that God created the heavens and the earth out of literally nothing yet He cannot preserve one book over two thousand years. God is sovereign and has created something that not only withstands the test of time but is living and can be applied to your life thousands of years after it was written! God's word is as true today as it was yesterday and will be that way for every tomorrow.

With all of these in mind, I encourage you to spend some time with God and ask that He help you uncover the answers within your own heart. Do not wait! For tomorrow may never come. Make the decision now to allow God to mold your life and destroy all the idols you have created.

To The Non Members

If you are not a member of any church, have never even thought about the true nature of God and what role He plays in your life, or do not really have any opinion one way or the other I urge you to set this book down and spend some time in humble prayer talking to Him. So many people forget that God is our Creator who desires a relationship with us and we can have an actual conversation with Him. Just like when you talk to a friend on the phone! Only this Friend knows everything about you, loves you more than you could ever imagine, and died to save you. Jesus can save you right where you are, right now. All you have to do is let Him in and He will grant you everlasting life.

Where ever you are in life I hope you can see that our focus should never be on us, our stuff, or any created thing. We are sinners badly in need of a savior, and it is only getting worse. Nothing we could do or will ever do will be worthy of worship. Honor, maybe, but not worship. Isaiah says that even our good deeds are as filthy rags (Isa. 64:6) in the eyes of the Lord. Instead, look for Jesus and find Him with open arms. He is a light that can lift you up when you are down, a rock when you need to be grounded and a comforter in times of need. I pray that when someone asks you "Where is Jesus?" you can respond humbly and lovingly, "In my heart."

If you have not given your life to Christ yet, can I just ask what you are waiting for? It is as easy as A, B, C. Just Admit you are a sinner in need of a savior. This should not be news to you. No matter how hard you try, you will continue to sin until you have taken your last breath. The "B" stands for believe. Believe that Jesus was a real person, who died for your sins as a perfect sacrifice. Lastly, "C" stands for choose. Simply **C**hoose to follow Him.

If you on the other hand are already a believer, I would urge you to pray with me and just ask God to be at his rightful place in your life.

Our Most Gracious and Loving Heavenly Father, thank you for Your grace and mercy. Thank you for sending Your Son to die in my stead. God, I pray that you search my heart and find the idols in my life that I have built an alter to. I so desperately desire to have You be the center of my life and I am ready and willing to make any changes necessary to put You there. Father, I pray that You grant me the strength to cast my idols at Your feet, right here, right now. Please Heavenly Father, find in me anything that has been blinding me from seeing You for who You really are. Help me to truly worship and honor You, now and every day forward. Amen.

Section Seven: My Journey to Christ

"You may forget that you are at every moment totally dependent on God."

-C. S. Lewis
Novelist, poet, and Christian apologist

I'd Like to Bare
My Testimony

Before I was saved I was lost. A lot of things in my life were going wrong and I was in a downward spiral. I realize how cliché that sounds, almost the cookie-cutter start of a testimony. However, in my case, it could not be more accurate. My life was literally in turmoil. Thankfully, on January 2, 2007 I accepted Christ as my Lord and Savior. It was a long, arduous journey, but its impact and importance remains immeasurable. The next chapter is my story, my conversion, my interaction with the true and living God. Christ saved me and I know He has the power to save anyone who tries to find Him.

From BC
to Born Again

I do not know if you have ever experienced a divorce, as a child or a participant. I hope not. Sadly, I and my family were not so lucky and as a result, felt its full effects. My parents were married a total of 23 years, and of those years I would say that a cumulative total of 2 years could be considered 'wedded bliss.' I do not know why they stayed together so long but in my opinion, they never should have married.

Since my parents' divorce was so involved, to save time and paper I will just give you the highlights. There were a few short-term (couple month) separations, a few court appearances, and various lawyers until they finally decided to call it quits just before my senior year of high school. During the divorce process tension was felt by everyone. Hatred saturated every word; whether it was from parent to child, child to parent, or sibling to sibling. Every day we had to strap on our armor just to walk around the house, shielding everyone from the true pain that was inside.

Sadly, my relationship with my mother was never top notch. In fact, ever since I reached the age of 12 it was rocky, at best. When my parents did finally divorce, our relationship went from bad to worse. We fought all the time during the transition and we had two really big fights that I can remember. Ultimately, it was these fights that ended up being the straw that broke the camel's back.

The first fight we had was over my first girlfriend. When I first told my mom about her, I was hoping she would be excited for me. Instead she told me I was not mature enough to handle a girlfriend. However, I did not see a problem. I had just turned 17, I was a 4.0 student, I was on the varsity football team, I was taking three advanced placement classes, and I was not on drugs. So I did what every teenager does, I asked dad. Luckily for me He said go for it. Looking back, I think he said it not only because he thought it was no big deal but he saw it as an opportunity to stick it to my mom. When she finally got word of my disobedience, she let into me for about an hour. At the end of the lecture, she told me to give her back my CTR ring. For those of you who are unfamiliar with that acronym, CTR stands for "Choose the Right." It is a saying that the Mormon Church uses, similar to the "What Would Jesus Do" (WWJD) slogan. This ring had been given to me on my birthday as a reminder to stay true to my faith. I was unaware that I could only wear it as long as I was deemed worthy. What was even more disheartening is that I am a big fan of male jewelry and I thought that having a Godly ring would be pretty cool. At that time I was still a practicing Mormon and the ring truly meant a lot to me. Despite my pleas, my mom told me that I, "was not acting Godly enough," and had to give it back. I took it off, placed it on the nightstand and walked out of the room. That was the last time I ever saw it.

The second fight was shortly after the ring fiasco. I forget why my mother and I were fighting, but we were. I only remember her standing in the doorway of my bedroom just grilling me for what I had done. In the middle of her berating me, she said, "I regret the day you were born." I went blank. Did she just say that to me? Did I hear her right? All I heard for a few seconds after that was similar to that of Charlie Brown's teacher: "wow wong wah, woh wah wong wong wah…" When my hearing normalized, I heard her say something to the effect of, "you're not my son."

That was it. From that moment on, I hated my mother. Our relationship to this day is in shambles. I have spoken to her a few times in passing, but as of right now we are not speaking nor have we spoken for several years.

With the divorce behind me, I was left heartbroken at the loss of my mother, my family, and my home. I started looking for an outlet to take the pain away, something to fill in the empty space that had formed. Playing guitar seemed an appropriate outlet.

I started a band my senior year with my best friend. He played bass, had the same sense of humor that I did, so it seemed a good fit. Soon enough we were writing song after song, most of which had very dark and emotionally charged lyrics. Writing music became very therapeutic for me. The first song I ever wrote was entitled "Down in Flames." It was about my battle with depression, with wanting to quit everything, and about how everyone who was once so dear to me had just simply turned their backs on me. More and more songs began to flow and I ended up with a little more than ten songs in a few months. The more I thought about how bad my life was, how hurt I was, how angry I was, the more songs we wrote.

During my family's divorce, my older brother had been on his LDS mission. He left before the divorce and came back to a broken home. I was excited for his return, mainly for two reasons. The first reason was because my brother is a pretty awesome guy and I was excited to be able to hang out with him again. The second reason was because he was a drummer in a band before he left on his mission and expressed a desire to be ours when he got home. After he got acclimated to our broken family state, he dusted off his drum set and our prayers for a drummer were answered. We jammed out a couple of songs and soon were in business. We were recording tons of songs and began booking show after show for any weekend we had available. It was the first time, in a long time, that I felt that I was on the path that I wanted to be on. I could finally be happy and put my bad days behind me. I felt important, like I was doing something meaningful. But it would not last...

Even though my newly formed band was on the rise, the relationship with my father was now beginning to wane. We fought almost every day, sometimes feeling as if it lasted all weekend. He was always on my case about everything and I honestly had a real hard time living with him. Looking back as an adult, I can now take some responsibility for some of the difficulties. I admit that I was irresponsible, indifferent, and calloused at times. However, some of the things my father told me during this time in my life, in my opinion, should never be said to a child. His remarks ranged from calling me worthless, to a screw up (sometimes with more colorful and explicit words), to a waste, as well as the all-encompassing "You'll never amount to anything!" cliché. He later told me that he was only trying to help me grow up, but all it did was make me feel unwanted and unloved. I began to carry this boulder of "screw-up" around my shoulders and every time something bad would happen, whether it was in the band or at home it was because of me. Suicide became not only a thought but a possibility.

The band was turning out to be not as fulfilling as one would hope and I soon looked to something else for comfort: women. Now I was never one to be single for long. In fact, since the start of my dating at the age of seventeen until I married at age twenty-three, I was single maybe a total of eight months. I sometimes dated girls just so I could have someone to talk to or someone to hold. I was not in a relationship for love, even though it felt that way most of the time. I was in it for me. I wanted someone to show off to the world, someone that would come to my gigs, feed my ego, and satisfy my lust. I did some things with these girls that were not honoring to God, myself, or them. To this day, I regret it.

God seemed to be slipping further and further off of my radar and I was not planning on putting Him back on any time soon. My life at the time was all about my band, my girlfriends, and my own desires. It was on my terms.

My faith in the LDS church, in God, and in the possibility of Heaven was diminishing, and so was my attendance. Occasionally I would go to a Mormon church looking for some fulfilment. The few times a year I did go I would generally enjoy myself but I never felt at home. I had Sundays where I would walk out of the LDS Church feeling on top of the world but by the time Monday rolled around that feeling had quickly faded. It was really weird. Instead of trying to force myself to enjoy church and be fed, I decided I would go whenever I felt the urge and let the chips fall where they may. I said to myself, as I had done several times before, "it will all work out in the end." I figured God, or whoever, would give me the desire to go back to church and then all the pieces would start fitting if that was where I was supposed to be. Then one day, my wavering religious belief took a huge hit and my world was turned upside down.

At around my twentieth birthday I found out that my parent's temple sealing had been broken. Mormons are married in one of their temples and are sealed for all time and eternity with their children. This means that in Heaven, a husband and wife can enjoy eternity with their children, and their children's children, and their children's children's children, etc. as one big happy family. I grew up being taught that the temple sealing is sacred and even in my weakened faith I was, apparently, still trusting that I would be with my family in Heaven. I found out that my mom wrote a few letters to the prophet and the stake president (the area manager of the church) which caused my dad to need to have a meeting with him. This meeting was to inform my dad that his and my mom's sealing was in jeopardy. My dad told me that he revealed to the stake president that he did not agree with this breakage and expressed his fear that my mom might possibly be bi-polar. He then asked to have the church rethink their decision. A few weeks later he got a letter in the mail stating that the church had decided to dissolve my parent's temple sealing. I remember wondering, "If God holds marriage in such high regard, why would He allow the leaders of His church nullify it?" Even though I hated my mom, I still wanted to be with her in Heaven. So did my dad. I remember thinking, "Why would God do this? Why would He allow His church to do this?"

Year after year would pass and the emotional roller coaster never seemed to stop. I would be bogged down because I was fighting with my dad or my siblings and then have a gig the next day and feel like a rock star. These emotional waves, coupled with the guilt of immorality, the thoughts of suicide, and my anger toward the Church, along with spurts of pure happiness was quite the ride.

One day, while my fellow band mates were watching TV, I felt like writing a song. So, I went out to the garage, grabbed my acoustic guitar and just started playing. Eventually, I wrote an acoustic ballad, very dark yet epic (if I may say so myself). I remember just thinking about my struggles with God, the church, and the difficulties over the past few years and I just started to write.

I feel like I've gone astray
But I was never shown the way
and now I walk on all alone
You were always there for me
then you turned your back on me
and now I'm stuck here wondering

Make me believe that all I've ever known is true
That it means something, that it means anything
What am I to do when I lack desire to aspire
lack commitment, will not listen
Cannot, I just cannot follow you

I know that I've done some wrong
but does that mean I can't go on
and live my life the way I choose

Just wash away my fears
Just wipe away my tears
Just wash away my fears

Now, the funny thing is, I never realized what I wrote until years later. This was a cry for help, directed at the Mormon Church. This was me asking for validation to my beliefs, asking if the past twenty years meant something. I wanted God to be real and the LDS church to be true but I just did not feel it anymore. At the time, I just thought I wrote a cool dark song. I did not see that my heart was actually crying out to God for help.

I will fast forward a bit, skipping a lot more of my "worldly" stories and tell you that it was during this time in my life where I felt like I was just treading water. It was a time when I had just ended a serious relationship with a girl that I almost proposed to. My friend and bandmate had some major issues to hash out. My relationship with my dad was in ruins. My relationship with my mom was still nonexistent. My band was slowly falling apart. My job was not fulfilling. I had no God, no religion, and I just did not care about anything anymore. I was taking a few college courses because I wanted to at least feel like I had accomplished something in my life, but since graduation was so far away, I just figured it would never happen. I just felt 'blah' in regards to everything going on around me. It was not that I was broke, or that I was into drugs or alcohol, but it was because I felt I had nothing in my life worthwhile. This is how I went through life for the next couple of weeks. I had a smile on the outside but a not much joy on the inside. Fortunately, I still had coordination. I loved playing any type of sport and around this time, it was another escape. Even when times got rough I was able to play or do something active to take my mind off of things. At that time volleyball was my outlet. I had been playing around two to three times a week for a few years and had actually gotten pretty good. Eventually I was invited by a friend to play at a local Christian church, namely High Desert Church (HDC). Honestly, location did not concern me. As long as I could play, it could be at my mom's house for all I cared.

I had been going to HDC's open gym for a few months, made some friends, and even had my eye on a few ladies, when I met Erlene. She was fun, lively, beautiful, and smart...I could go on and on...literally. After about a week of flirting I got up the nerve to ask her out. She asked me if I was a Christian, to which I quickly responded, "Yes." (I thought I was, as do most Mormons). After a wonderful night of getting to know each other, I got her number and we started going out. In the weeks that followed, we would talk on the phone for hours on end and go on dates whenever we could. It was not long until I realized that I was falling more and more in love with her.

Though we both considered ourselves Christians, we quickly found out that our theologies were very different. After a month or so of dating, and after she and I had already developed strong feelings for one another, we got to the heart of our ever increasing disconnect. I do not quite remember how it happened, I just remember her saying that she considered herself a Southern Baptist and I said I was a Mormon.

This was a problem. She told me that she was not allowed to date a man who was not a Christian, to which I replied, "Well I am!" After a long discussion we decided to continue to date under the assumption that we could never be more than boyfriend and girlfriend until we were equally yoked. I loved this girl quite a bit and I thought that if I just hung on long enough she would see the error of her ways and realize that it is not that big of a deal. So I said, okay. She also asked if I would be willing to come to church with her once in a while. Again, since I had no real ties to any religion, I thought I would play her game for a while. Worst case scenario is I waste a few hours of my day.

So I attended her Baptist Church a few times a month. Occasionally the pastor would say something that clashed with my Mormon theology and I would perk up. I have never been one to shy away from my feelings and I would ever so quietly whisper in her ear, "that's not right" or, "that's not how it happened" or, "God's not like that." She would just smile back at me and nod as if to say, "Well, that's not what I believe." Eventually I started to really listen to these sermons. Things the pastor was saying were clearly not Mormon theology but it was starting to make sense. The more I went to church with her, the more questions I would have. It did not take long until I realized that I needed to get some answers for myself.

At this time we had been dating for about a year. I do not remember what Erlene and I were talking about but the topic of marriage came up. We had gotten very close and truly loved one another and I thought that maybe I had worn her down. We talked about the prospect of us getting married and where we would live, you know, cheesy stuff. Then we started talking about important issues, like where our kids would go to church. I said that because I still was not close to God, they could go with her and I would either stay home or go to my church. She said that she still wanted a unified family in Christ. She then told me that she wanted a husband that would help her and her kids grow in God, not just one that exists. She wanted the strong patriarch type. She also reiterated that it would be a sin for us to be married if we were not equally yoked.

I saw her face and knew how important God was to her. Then and there I decided to see if the whole God thing was right for me. But, since I had not yet gotten an answer yet as to whether or not I should go to the Mormon Church, that is where I decided to start. I figured that was what I knew so why not start there?

I started attending a few scripture classes at the local LDS institute building. It was taught by a man that I still love and respect today. To keep him anonymous, I will call him Brother Johnson. I call him "Brother" because that is how I knew him. First names are rarely used in the Mormon Church. Everyone calls each other Brother or Sister coupled with their last name. He was a nice guy, always eager and happy to answer any and all of my questions. I must have asked him at least a dozen questions ranging from salvation to creation in a week. I would even ask my brother, the return missionary, a question every once in a while. He was, as far as I was concerned, an expert in Mormon theology. He was a highly respected missionary, very well versed and well spoken, and seemed to have a wealth of knowledge. Any question I would bring to him I would get an in depth answer with scripture for support. With all of these LDS resources at my fingertips I began to believe that Mormonism was in fact very true.

The longer Erlene and I stayed together, the more and more I dove into my religious studies. Occasionally, we would talk about marriage and kids and how to raise them. Only now my position had changed. I did not want to just pawn my kids off and let them go to her church. I wanted them to be Mormon; I wanted my wife to be Mormon. I began to discuss visitation rights regarding my non-existent kids to my prospective wife. I would say, "you can have them on the first and third Sundays, and I'll take the other ones and we'll let our kids decide for themselves when they get older." Erlene would always reply with a deafening, "No. That's just not going to work."

I realized what I had to do. I had to prove to Erlene that Mormonism was right. My studies became more focused on proselytizing than anything else. I was going to convert this girl and marry her in the temple! Purpose driven, I needed answers. I would ask Brother Johnson or my brother specific questions, and armed with the answer I would take it to Erlene and try to convert her. These debates seemed to take over our date nights. Very quickly she felt the need to add a stipulation to our debates. We could discuss theology as long as we did not argue or fight about it. Once a debate became heated or hostile, she would say, "that's it, I'm done. This is not how to do this."

So we would discuss anything and everything. Oddly enough, no matter what I brought to her, she always seemed to be able to soundly prove me wrong, biblically. I would walk away frustrated and eager to find more answers. Time and time again, the result was the same. I thought that maybe I just did not have enough information. I thought that if I studied more the tables would soon turn.

At this point, I was now attending two churches: mine and hers. However, one good thing about going to her church was that I would be able to enjoy a free lunch with her at her parent's or parent's friend's home. Permit me to tell you a bit about them. They are the most amazing people you will ever meet, and I am not saying that just because they will probably read this. I really mean it.

They of course knew that I was LDS and I, of course, knew that they did not approve of us dating. However, they were always very welcoming, loving, and cheerful to me. I had a suspicion that they were all fake, that this was all just an act. I just knew that they were holding out and acting nice until Erlene wised up and found someone better.

When I first met her mom, she was kind, but reserved. I knew she knew all about me and I just figured it was because she did not know how to act around me yet. Her dad was a local Baptist pastor and when he found out I was Mormon his response was to give me a book. It was written by an ex-Mormon and it was his journey to Christianity. I respectfully took the book, smiled and thanked him knowing I would never read it, and then tossed it under a pile of clothes when I got home. Her brothers were cool guys but it was really hard to feel comfortable around them simply because of our infrequent meetings. They lived on their own and were only around for holidays or whatnot. However, whenever they were around I always felt like they were judging me for some reason. This actually became the topic of several arguments between the two of us on several occasions. Even though they were always very nice to me, I still felt their disapproving eyes burning a hole in me and I resented them for it. I did not realize until later that my uncomfortableness was a result of my low self-esteem. I still felt like I was not worth anything. I would put myself in their shoes and hate that my little sister was dating such a loser. Erlene would tell me over and over again that her brothers were just concerned for both of us, but I struggled believing her. Luckily, the more and more I hung out with all of them, the more and more I realized they were all very genuine people. Eventually I felt completely at ease and enjoyed their company.

Even Erlene's family friends were amazing. I still remember the first time I met them. It was July 4th, 2005 and I was invited to their house for a barbecue. At first I felt awkward but that feeling quickly faded. The more and more I hung out with them, the more and more these people astounded me. I felt honestly loved. They made me feel important and respected, and their joy was infectious.

I started to look forward to Sundays. Church became a joy for me, which is something that I was not used to. The pastor was now frequently making sense and instead of mockingly saying, "that's wrong" I would earnestly ask "is that right?" I found myself seeking out the pastor after church services to ask him questions. I still sought the counsel of Brother Johnson from time to time, but our visits were becoming less and less. I stopped asking my brother any Mormon questions and was attending the Mormon Church less and less.

As I said, going to church with Erlene brought me happiness. However, one service in particular I got a taste of what it was like to have joy. The praise team was playing the song "Lifesong" by Casting Crowns. Erlene had introduced me to a few Christian bands before, but being the metal head that I am, they really did not interest me much. However this song was different. Although there was no screaming, no screeching guitars, and no pounding drums, it was a breath of fresh air. It was the lyrics that spoke to me. "Make my lifesong sing to You!" This is what my heart was yearning for all this time. I wanted to live for God but as of yet I just did not know how. It was as if this song was written especially for me. I immediately wanted the CD because I wanted to feel this close to Him all the time. So her being the awesome girlfriend that she is, she went out and bought me a Casting Crowns CD.

God was working wonders in me. My heart was changing. My life was getting better but I still did not know Him personally. Luckily, God was not finished with me. At this time, Erlene and I had been dating now for about a year and a half and marriage seemed to be the next logical step. I knew though we could never get married as long as we were unequally yoked. I needed to find out where God fit into my life once and for all. I knew that I could no longer string Erlene along.

One day, I woke up with a strange desire to read. I say strange because I hate reading, literally. It is amazing that I passed my English classes in high school, let alone wrote this book, because of how much I hate to read. This day, however, was different. I needed to read. I even went as far as to try and make plans to go to the library or Barnes and Noble to buy a book. I suppose that I just wanted to be intellectual for a change or something. I asked Erlene if she had any books I could read, not too long of course, let's not get crazy. I just wanted something to wet my whistle. She mentioned a few titles but nothing of real interest to me.

That evening, after I returned home from work, I walked into my room and saw the gigantic mess that was before me. I decided it was time for a nice, thorough cleaning. I hoped that it might take my mind off of things and help me unwind. As I started to put clothes away, and wipe off dirt stains from the wall, I noticed a thin, baby-blue book I had not seen for months. It was the book Erlene's dad gave me when I first met him years earlier, entitled Beyond Mormonism, by James R. Spencer. It is the story of a highly respected Mormon who, after searching the scriptures and finding certain things out, ended up leaving the church and becoming a Christian. I was intrigued because this was exactly where I was in life. I too was still searching the Mormon Church for answers. I picked it up, dusted it off, and immediately looked at how many pages it had. (I told you, I hate reading.) Since it was under two-hundred pages I decided to start reading the book.

That night I was only able to read a few chapters before I had to go to bed, but when I awoke the next morning it was the first thing I grabbed. I read some more as I was getting ready for work and all throughout the day I kept finding ways to get away so I could read. Even when I got off work, hours later, I still could not put it down. I was reading and pondering on my drive home, catching paragraphs between lights. When I got home, I immediately sat on my bed and kept on reading.

It was sort of eerie at times, because this man was me. Every confusing thing he encountered, every question he could not find answers to, every problem the Mormon Church dealt him, I was dealt too in some ways. He mentioned things about his broken family and how the church dealt with him, which echoed a painful sound in my heart. He revealed several other experiences that he had in the Mormon Church that I felt were unique only to my situation. I do not remember the exact moment I started to cry. I just remember noticing droplets on the page. I thought all of my problems with the Mormon Church were because I was too stupid to understand the doctrine, or that my life was so convoluted that I was the special case, or that maybe I was too stubborn or naïve to see the truth. In that moment, I quickly realized the sad reality: the LDS church was not what I was raised to believe it was.

In his book, James R. Spencer quoted scripture references in the Book of Mormon that were contradictory to what the Holy Bible said. This was news to me because I was raised that the Bible and the Book of Mormon went "hand in hand." So, I whipped out my Triple Combination (Book of Mormon, Pearl of Great Price, and Doctrine and Covenants) and my Bible and checked every single one of his references. To my amazement, he was right. The more and more I read, the more and more I knew God was reaching out to me.

I ended up finishing the book at around 2:00am. With all of his resources checked, all of my fears and doubts about Mormonism confirmed, I knew I did not know God but I so desperately wanted to.

I decided to call Erlene. I knew it was late but I also knew it could not wait. With my eyes glazed over and my nose stopped up, I dialed. After a few rings she groggily answered. I do not remember the entire conversation verbatim. But I do know that it went something like this:

"Hello?"

"Hey babe, it's me."

"Are you okay?"

"Yeah, I'm fine. Sorry for calling so late."

"That's okay, what's up?"

"I...I don't want to be Mormon anymore."

"Okay...?"

"I just read that book your dad gave me and I realized I need Jesus. I need God."

"Oh baby! Praise God!"

"I called you because I don't know how to get Him. What do I do?

"Just pray, and ask Him into your heart."

That night I was saved. At two o'clock in the morning, she led me to my knees and I accepted Christ. I admitted that I was a sinner and that I needed Christ to save me. I do not know how long I prayed, a few minutes or so probably, but when I was done I knew I was saved. I knew that God had forgiven all of my sins and that I was safely in His grace. I knew I had made the right choice. I did not know what the future would hold but I knew that I could hold on to God and He would get me through anything.

Looking back, it is funny how God gets a hold of you. God was molding me to hear His voice, to see His truth, in every step I took. When women were my main focus, He sent me a woman to change my focus to Him. When my family was breaking apart, God placed amazing, loving people in my life to help me get through it. When my band left a void, God filled it with uplifting Christian music. No matter what life threw at me, God made sure that I was taken care of.

He knew I would hide that book until I was ready to find Him. I am a firm believer in the phrase "In God's time." How awesome is it to know that the creator of the heavens and the earth loves us so much that He would orchestrate people's lives to be perfectly interwoven so that we can find Him. God was working wonders in my life and I could not be more joyful about the outcome. Even though I could not see Him, He was there during my pain all along. He was waiting for me all that time to turn and run to him.

After I converted, my relationship with Erlene only grew stronger. I eventually did the smart thing and asked her to marry me. With her parents' approval, and Erlene's consent, we were married that October.

I have since joined a new band. I am playing every chance I get for my church's worship team. Take my word for it; playing for Him is a lot more rewarding than playing for yourself. I have cut back on my secular music, and listen primarily to Christian Rock. However, every once in a while I will still throw in a Metallica CD, just to mix it up a bit.

My family life has gotten better as well, thanks be to God. My relationship with my dad may not be perfect, but it is better now and I love him dearly. He and I have come leaps and bounds from where we once were. My brothers, sisters, and I are closer than ever before, and it is getting better every day. Of course, not every problem is fixed but my joy is still full. I just try to let them know every chance I get that I truly love them and I know that they love me.

My mom and I still have not really talked since the divorce. I have made some efforts to repair the damage, even took her out to lunch a few times and even invited her to my wedding, but nothing has changed. However, I do believe in the power of God and I know He can restore all things. So, I will wait patiently and prayerfully for God to heal that which is broken.

God is awesome, and not a day goes by that I do not thank him for what He did in me. I hope and pray that you know just how great our God truly is. If you do not have a relationship with Jesus Christ, I hope that maybe one day God will throw you a curve ball, and put a little Jesus in your life.

Acknowledgements

"Give thanks in all circumstances; for this is the will of God in Christ Jesus for you."

-1 Thessalonians 5:18

In preparing this book, there are a few people that I would like to specifically acknowledge for their work. These people played more of a major role in inspiring me, educating me, and helping me in my ministry to reach the LDS community and write this book.

James R. Spencer – Author – for his book entitled "Beyond Mormonism: An Elder's Story."
www.beyondmormonism.com

Dr. Walter Ralston Martin – Founder of Christian Research Institute – for his lecture entitled "Maze of Mormonism."
www.youtube.com/user/WalterMartinDotCom

Shawn McCraney – Founder of the TV show "Heart of the Matter" – for his many debates and informative episodes on his show.
http://hotm.tv/

Aaron Shafovaloff – Mormonism Research Ministry – for his views on God's sinless nature.
www.youtube.com/user/aaronshaf2006

I would also like to thank Pastor Earl Lanting and Pastor Todd Arnett for their assistance in making sure the Biblical perspective in this book is true and accurate. I am not a Bible scholar and could not have done this without your help. I want to also thank my lovely wife Erlene for her help and support. Lastly, I want to thank my Lord and Savior Jesus Christ for His direction, grace, and love.